C000139630

THIS BOOK
BELONGS TO

Barbara Russell

2am. Rolling Home

FOLLOWING THE DAY-TO-DAY EVENTS OF BARBARA RUSSELL
AS A YOUNG WOMAN AND NURSE, HER EVERYDAY LIFE AND TRAVELS
RECORDED IN A FIVE YEAR HAND WRITTEN DIARY
1946-1950 IN POST-WAR BRITAIN

Front cover: Montage of original diary, photographs and ephemera.
Endpapers: written excerpts from original diary.

for

AMY, JON, STEPHANIE,
ZOË, MICHAEL & LIAM

Original diary hand written by Barbara Russell.
Reproduced, compiled and recreated by Sarah Louise Booth.
Copyright © Sarah Louise Booth © slb1 2014
Published by slb1publishing.
www.slb1publishing.com

This book has been typeset in Garamond Light Condensed Italic
and Copperplate Gothic Condensed BT & Bold Condensed BT.

Printed by slb1publishing

ISBN
Hardback 978-0-9562614-0-3

All rights reserved
No part of this publication may be produced or transmitted in
any form or by any means, electronic or mechanical, including
photocopying, recording or any information storage or retrieval
system, without permission in writing from publisher.

Contents

FIVE YEAR DIARY

WHEN CLEARING OUT THE LOFT OF MY FAMILY HOME MANY YEARS AGO I FOUND AN OLD, ANTIQUE WRITING BOX. INSIDE WAS A SMALL, LEATHER BOUND, FIVE YEAR HAND WRITTEN DIARY BY MY LATE MOTHER. IMMERSING MYSELF IN THIS WONDERFUL, HIDDEN GEM I READ THROUGH IT COMPLETELY ABSORBED AND FASCINTATED. IT WAS A VERY BITTER-SWEET MOMENT AND I SENTIMENTALLY PUT IT AWAY FOR SAFE KEEPING BUT NEVER QUITE FORGETTING ITS EXISTENCE.

THE DIARY FOLLOWS HER DAY-TO-DAY ROUTINES AS A YOUNG WOMAN AND NURSE RECORDED BETWEEN 1946-1950 IN POST WAR BRITAIN. IT STARTS HUMOROUSLY WITH HERSELF (BARB) AND HER CLOSE COMPANION NANCE, CELEBRATING THE BEGINNING OF 1946 AFTER THE GRIM WAR YEARS. THERE ARE REFERENCES TO THE MIDDLESEX HOSPITAL IN LONDON WHERE SHE TRAINED AND WORKED, FORESTER HILLS IN ABERDEEN AND MOUNT VERNON HOSPITAL AT NORTHWOOD PARK. WITH BARB/BABS AS SHE WAS SO OFTEN KNOWN, LIVING AT PLACES SUCH AS FULHAM, PUTNEY, WEDMORE IN SOMERSET, MAIDENHEAD, EDINBURGH AND ABERDEEN.

INITIALLY ONLY INTENDING TO PRODUCE 'A PIECE OF FAMILY HISTORY' I BECAME ENGROSSED IN THE DETAIL AND THE RESULT IS '2AM, ROLLING HOME' WHICH INCLUDES ALL THE ORIGINAL HAND WRITTEN CONTENT LINKED TO RELEVANT PHOTOGRAPHS FROM HER OWN ALBUMS OF THE STAFF, BUILDINGS AND PATIENTS WHO WERE PRESENT AT THOSE HOSPITALS DURING THAT TIME, ALONG WITH HER NURSING COLLEAGUES AND FRIENDS MENTIONED.

FOREWORD

A SECTION ON THE NHS IN PRE AND POST WAR BRITAIN HAS BEEN INCLUDED AND ADDITIONALLY, I HAVE PLACED BOTH FACTUAL AND HISTORICAL SNIPPETS ALONGSIDE THE DIARY ENTRIES. TUBERCULOSIS, THE 'WHITE PLAGUE' HAS BEEN INCLUDED AND IS ALSO RELEVANT. I WAS LUCKY ENOUGH TO VISIT THE MIDDLESEX HOSPITAL BEFORE IT WAS SOLD OFF AND REBUILT AS PRIVATE APARTMENTS. OBTAINING INFORMATION FROM THE ARCHIVIST I WAS ABLE TO VIEW MY MOTHER'S PTS (PRELIMINARY TRAINING SCHOOL) RECORDS. SOME OF THE ORIGINAL WARD NAMES AT THE MIDDLESEX MENTIONED IN THE DIARY NO LONGER EXIST, SUCH AS ROSALIND CHETWYND BUT I WAS FORTUNATE IN FINDING SOMEONE WHO DID REMEMBER THEM.

WITH TRAVEL BEING ALLOWED AFTER WWII AND THE RE-ISSUE OF PASSPORTS I MAPPED THE JOURNEY'S THAT SHE UNDERTOOK WITH HER FRIENDS AND NURSING COLLEAGUES ON CYCLING AND YOUTH HOSTELING TRIPS TO SCOTLAND, DENMARK, COPENHAGEN AND SWEDEN.

OTHER FASCINATING ENTRIES INVOLVE THE SILVER WEDDING CELEBRATIONS OF THE THEN KING AND QUEEN, THE 1948 OLYMPIC GAMES, SKATING SESSIONS, THEATRE, CINEMA AND FILM TRIPS, TEA AND COFFEE HOUSES AND READING PENGUIN BOOKS.

THE DIARY ENDS ON A NOTE OF SADNESS BUT ALSO ONE OF NEW BEGINNINGS.

All you that in my life have been,
All you that are,
You that are now but known in dream
Dwelling afar,
And you the star
Of every hour, the living gleam
That lights my earth-ways into Heaven
To you is this book humbly given.

1904 - 1936 Poems, Lord Gorell, First Edition January 15, 1937 MCMXXXVII.

Prior to World War II British industry was in a period of recovery after an era of poverty and mass unemployment during the 1930s. This was due to the country rearming in readiness for war. German troops had invaded Poland and subsequently Britain and France were at war with Germany. Rationing had started and Winston Churchill invited the Labour Party to join his wartime coalition government. A report was drawn up by social reformer William Beveridge in order to implement a plan for care ~ The Welfare State, partly funded by National Insurance contributions and taxes. After the War the world was in a

1939
- WORLD WAR II BEGINS AFTER HITLER INVADES POLAND

1940
- RATIONING STARTS IN THE UK
- CHURCHILL BECOMES PRIME MINISTER OF BRITAIN
- THE PENSION AGE FOR WOMEN IS REDUCED TO 60 YEARS

HISTORICAL AND SOCIAL EVENTS DURING 1939-1945
Extracts from ~ *Chronology of British History,* Brockhampton Reference.

1941
- CONSCRIPTION FOR SINGLE WOMEN AGE 20-30, UP TO AGE 43 FOR MARRIED WOMEN. EXEMPT WERE PREGNANT WOMEN & YOUNG CHILDREN
- TRADES UNION CONGRESS PLEDGES EQUAL PAY
- AMY JOHNSON DIES AFTER CRASHING INTO THE THAMES IN THE CARGO PLANE SHE WAS PILOTING FOR THE ATA, (AIR TRANSPORT AUXILIARY)

desperate condition. Cities lay in ruins. Millions were homeless. Japan was laid waste by fire bombs and two atomic bombs. Germany was occupied by the Allies ~ British, French, American and Russian troops. Everyone was grateful for peace and though for some it was a long process, countries began to pick themselves up. The Government, now led by Clement Attlee began to carry out major changes and reconstruction in Britain. Many hospitals, the Bank of England, railways, road-haulage, civil aviation, gas, electricity and the coal and steel industries were nationalized. State benefits and pensions were increased and the National Health Service, was started to provide everyone with free medical care.

1942

- THE CHURCH OF ENGLAND RELAXES RULE ON WOMEN WEARING HATS TO CHURCH
- THE POST OFFICE TAKES ON 5,000 WOMEN ENGINEERS

AND GARMENT WORKERS UNION SINCE 1915

- PHYLLIS DEAKIN, TIMES JOURNALIST, FIRST MEETING OF WOMAN'S PRESS CLUB IN A PUB IN FLEET STREET

1943

- BANDLEADER IVY BENSON AND 'GIRLS', FIRST APPEARANCE AS BBC'S RESIDENT DANCE BAND
- DAME ANNE LOUGHLIN, FIRST WOMAN PRESIDENT OF TUC. ORGANISER FOR THE TAILORS

1944

- 'D' DAY. ALLIED LANDING, NORMANDY COAST
- BAN ON WOMEN TEACHERS' MARRYING LIFTED
- 13TH MODERN OLYMPIC GAMES CANCELLED IN LONDON

The Education Act was implemented, raising the school leaving age to 15, providing free secondary and further education. A series of Acts provided insurance for every major form of need and a free leaflet service for everyone.

Only those who have lived through the between-war years can appreciate the social revolution brought about by this legislation. Britain was impoverished and exhausted, the period of the labour government was inevitably one of austerity, when rationing was even more stringent than during the war. Imports were discouraged and exports encouraged. Slowly a trade revival began and yet many of the effects of World War II lasted nearly half a century.

1945

- 'VE' DAY, GERMANY SURRENDERS
- LABOUR WINS THE ELECTION, CLEMENT ATTLEE BECOMES PRIME MINISTER
- 'RED' ELLEN WILKINSON BECOMES FIRST WOMAN MINISTER OF EDUCATION
- THE AMERICANS DROP AN ATOM BOMB ON HIROSHIMA
- VICTORY OVER JAPAN DAY MARKS THE END OF WWII
- DAME KATHLEEN LONSDALE, CRYSTALLOGRAPHER AND MARJORY STEPHENSON, BACTERIOLOGIST, ELECTED AS FIRST WOMEN FELLOWS BY THE ROYAL SOCIETY
- FAMILY ALLOWANCE INTRODUCED, CAMPAIGN LED BY ELEANOR RATHBONE
- THEATRE DIRECTOR, JOAN LITTLEWOOD SETS UP LEFT-WING THEATRE WORKSHOP
- PUBLICATION OF BRIDESHEAD REVISITED BY EVELYN WAUGH
- UNITED NATIONS COMES INTO EXISTENCE

A Ministry of Health, established in 1919 brought together medical and public health functions of central government, co-ordinating and supervising local health services in England and Wales. Its responsibilities covered the powers and duties in relation to the Poor Laws, health of mothers, treatment of school children, limited health insurance, environmental health factors such as water, housing, sewerage, town planning, mental health and preventative and curative medicine. The Ministry made improvements in areas such as adoption, tackling smoking, housing (a traditional cause of ill health), public health, food and medicines as well as offering advice to voluntary hospitals, which provided most medical training.

In 1928 the Ministry published a White Paper that took the first steps towards a better organised health care system. Before the creation of the NHS, people often went without medical treatment, relying instead on sometimes dangerous or dubious

- 1919 MINISTRY OF HEALTH ESTABLISHED
- 1928 MINISTRY OF HEALTH PUBLISHED WHITE PAPER - FIRST STEPS
- 1942 BEVERIDGE REPORT - SOCIAL INSURANCE & ALLIED SERVICES
- 1944 MINISTRY OF HEALTH PUBLISHED WHITE PAPER
- 1946 NATIONAL HEALTH SERVICE ACT AND NEW TOWNS ACT
- 1948 NATIONAL HEALTH SERVICE (NHS) ESTABLISHED

remedies or on the charity of doctors who gave their services free to their poorest patients. Alongside hospitals charging for services, there were charitable and voluntary hospitals, which tended to deal mainly with serious illnesses. The local authorities of large towns provided municipal hospitals ~ maternity, hospitals for infectious diseases like smallpox and tuberculosis, as well as hospitals for the elderly, mentally ill and mentally handicapped. The Second World War highlighted the lack of proper co-ordination of health services, the duplications and gaps in services that were being provided by 3,000 autonomous institutions. This led to a co-ordinated wartime Emergency Hospital Service and planning for peacetime services that laid the foundation for a national planned service.

In 1942 the Beveridge Report (Social Insurance and Allied Services) was published. The report proposed a weekly national insurance contribution in return for benefits paid to the sick, unemployed, retired or widowed. It proposed that: "medical treatment covering all requirements will be provided for all citizens by a national health service organised under the health departments and post-medical rehabilitation treatment will be provided for all persons capable of profiting by it."

The Report was followed by a White Paper in 1944 and the National Health Service Act 1946 that led to the establishment *of the National Health Service (NHS) on 1 July 1948. With the creation of the NHS the Ministry changed its role from a regulator to a manager of a unified health system, consisting of two ministers and around 2,700 civil servants. The years after the war saw intensive development within the international pharmaceutical industry, including the introduction of penicillin and modern vaccines. A founding principle of the NHS was that it should improve health and prevent disease, not just provide treatment for those who are ill.*

On 5 July 1948 the National Health Service became reality. It was a momentous achievement and everybody wanted the new service to work. However, food was still rationed, building materials were short and there was a shortage of fuel. The war had created a housing crisis, alongside post war rebuilding of cities and the designation of overspill areas, the New Towns Act (1946) created major new centres of population and all needed health services.

The NHS brought hospital services, GP's, family practitioner services (doctors, pharmacists, opticians and dentists) and community based services into an integrated and organised service that provided healthcare for the first time, for the whole population. It was not easy holding everything together.

Keeping everyone on board continued to create administrative difficulties for years. Financial problems, however, were worse. It was impossible to predict the day to day costs of the new service and public expectations rose. Medical science was rapidly gathering pace, hospital beds for tuberculosis were closed, allowing cash to be released for other services. More mothers were wanting their babies delivered in hospital, cardiac surgery was being applied to rheumatic heart disease and hip replacements were beginning to be performed. Initial estimates of the cost of the NHS were soon exceeded as newer, more expensive and more frequently used drugs were developed.

Within three years of its creation, the NHS, which had been conceived as free of direct charges for everyone, was forced to introduce some modest fees. Prescription charges of one shilling (5p), which had been legislated for as early as 1949 but not implemented, were introduced in 1952. A flat rate of £1 for ordinary dental treatment was brought in as well.

Many of the tensions that emerged in the early days of the NHS have challenged its senior management and successive Governments ever since.

Extracts taken from ~ *A Concise History of England*, F E Haliday.
Department of Health, Government UK website: www.gov.uk
Health Services before 1948: www.nhs.uk

The second World War began, as far as the Middlesex was concerned in May 1939 when with other hospitals it took the initiative in planning an emergency Medical Service. Suffering air attacks in 1940, 41 and 44. The first flying bombs arrived a few days after 'D' day, June 44 with many hits close to the hospital. All casualties were brought to the hospital. There was an underground operating theatre prepared for use during the war for the treatment of air raid casualties. The wounded would be first treated at the Middlesex and then tranferred to other hospitals, such as Mount Vernon Hospital at Northwood, Tindal House at Aylesbury, Stoke Mandeville at Aylesbury and St Andrews at Dollis Hill.

During the war years time was still found for research work into such problems as the treatment of burns, the crush syndrome in air-raid casualties, the supply of calcium and the chemistry of certain important glands in the human body.

Although the nurses home in Foley Street and Cleveland Street was close by, many nurses not on duty, slept in the sub basement surrounded by their most treasured possessions, including suitcases filled with houshold linen for those engaged to be married. The exemplary conduct of the nurses was in no small measure due to the precepts given and the example set by Matron Dorothy Smith. Her influence was profound and she

Babs (Barbara) relaxing off duty on the roof of The Middlesex, with one of the many hospital cats

LINE DRAWING TAKEN FROM THE COVER OF 'THE MIDDLESEX HOSPITAL', 'THE NAMES OF THE WARDS AND THE STORY THEY TELL', C D SHAW & W R WINTERTON, PUBLISHED BY THE FRIENDS OF THE MIDDLESEX HOSPITAL

*did much to mould the modern Middlesex Hospital nurse. The
Middlesex has always paid particular attention to the care and
well-being of their nurses, from Sarah Whittaker appointed in
1746 to the two hundred student nurses annually admitted
to the full status of nurses two centuries later.*

*Until the passing of the National Health Act in 1946 and the
founding of the National Health Service in 1948 The Middlesex
was financed entirely by voluntary subscriptions and donations.*

Extracts from *The Middlesex Hospital*, Hilary St. George Saunders.

CHAIRMAN 1938-1946 THE HON JOHN J ASTOR, COLONEL

RESIDENT MEDICAL OFFICER ALFRED E WEBB JOHNSTON 1880-1958,
VICE PRESIDENT OF HOSPITAL 1941. FIRST MEMBER OF THE MEDICAL
TEAM TO HAVE A WARD NAMED AFTER HIM WHILE STILL ON ACTIVE STAFF

PHYSICIANS/SURGEONS G GORDON TAYLOR 1907-1946, ALFRED E WEBB
JOHNSON 1911-1946, W TURNER WARWICK 1923-1949, R VAUGHAN
HUDSON 1928 *onw*, E W RICHES 1930 *onw*, D H PATEY 1930 *onw*, P B
ASCROFT 1937 *onw*, R S HANDLEY 1946 *onw*, C J B MURRAY 1946 *onw*.

PHYSICIAN/ACCOUCHEURS VICTOR BONNEY 1908-1937

OBSTETRIC & GYNAECOLOGICAL SURGEONS L CARNAC RIVETT
1930-1947, F W ROQUES 1930 *onw*, W R WINTERTON 1938 *onw*,
I M JACKSON 1948 *onw*.

PHYSICIANS & SURGEONS TO SPECIAL DEPARTMENTS/ANAESTHETISTS
B R M JOHNSON 1936 *onw*, F W ROBERTS 1939-1949, O P DINNICK 1946
B A SELLICK 1946 *onw*, A J H HEWER 1948 *onw*.

MATRONS MISS D M SMITH 1929 *onw*, MISS M MARRIOTT 1946 *onw*.

SECRETARIES BRIGADIER G P HARDY-ROBERTS 1946 *onw*.

'... A CORNER OF MY SITTING ROOM'

SISTER: 'JUST ABOUT TO GO ON DUTY'

20

THE MIDDLESEX — PRELIMINARY TRAINING SCHOOL

NAME: BARBARA RUSSELL,
PAGE 194/12, NO. 427, P72
DATE OF ADMISSION: 28.12.42.
DATE OF TRANSFER: 22.3.43
W.P.A.L. M.O.L.27.2.43 193-6
RUSSELL BARBARA 28.12.42
NO. 386 PTS PRELIMINARY
TRAINING SCHOOL 1943
XXX IN P.T.S.

*Preliminary Training School
Records,* Trust Archivist, UCLH.

TOP ROW - UNKNOWN,
BOTTOM ROW L/R
- ISABELLE, BARBARA,
PENNY/PERRY

1943 MARCH 22ND S STOKE
MANDEVILLE L AND J (WORTH
& EYES)
APRIL 25TH S STOKE MANDEVILLE
3X (M.MED)
JUNE 21ST HOLIDAY 12 DAYS
JULY 5TH S STOKE MANDEVILLE
JULY 8TH S STOKE MANDEVILLE
JULY 10TH S STOKE MANDEVILLE
(WORTH & EYES) PN
OCT 4TH HOLIDAY 12 DAYS
OCT 13TH
OCT 26TH 3 (CHILD)
NOV 1ST TO THE MIDDLESEX, KING
GEO — (M SUNG) B
1944 JAN 10
JAN 14 ILL CONJUNCTIVIVTUS
FEB 16TH BRODENTS (WOMPS
& BEFORE)
14TH ILL AT HOME COLD
18TH PR. ARTHUR M.LUNG: RELIEF
28TH HOLIDAY — 2 WEEKS
MARCH 14TH CASUALTY: BIO: CHEM
APRIL 10TH
APRIL 20TH PR. AULTEEN
M.LUNG) SUPER
JUNE 5TH TRANSFERRED TO
ALVERSTOKE HOSPITAL SERVICE
WOUNDED. N.
JULY 26TH TRANSFERRED TO THE
MIDDLESEX HOSPITAL
HOLIDAY — 2 WEEKS
AUG 9TH OUT PATIENTS. D
OCT 10TH

NOV 1ST. TRANSFERRED TO
MOUNT VERNON HOSPITAL,
HUT 22 (WHED: NEMON & SKIN)
NOV 26TH HUT 18 (M.LUNG: OENT)
DEC 18TH (SERVICE WOUNDED)
1945 JAN 1ST
FEB 14TH. HOLIDAY 2 WEEKS
FEB 15TH THEATRE
MARCH 26TH
APRIL 7TH HUT 20 (M.MED: HEMO)
MAY 19TH TO THE MIDDLESEX
HOSPITAL. WEBB JOHNSON
(M LUNG P.T)
MAY 22ND WOOL: WING 2ND N
JUNE 25TH
2. SEPT 1ST Q ALEX (GYNOR) D PL
SEPT 10TH HOLIDAY 2 WEEKS
4. SEPT 24 Q ALEX
DEC 8TH MATERNITY WARD PL
DEC 21ST-24TH, HOLIDAY 2 WEEKS
1946 JAN 4TH ESS. IVY. C. SAND
HEAD. SENG. PT JAN 12TH
MAR:18 W. JOHN & F. ASTOR
IN ACT/SICK
MAR: 26
JUNE 15TH TRANSFERRED
& MOUNT VERNON HOSPITAL
HUT 20 (M.MEDICAL)
JUNE 24TH
AUG 26TH HOLIDAY 2 WEEKS
SEPT 9TH HUT 22 (.NEURO
& SKINS)
1947 LEFT. JANUARY 12TH
TRAINING COMPLETED

17.6.43 PASSED NURSING COMMITTEE
1943 SEPTEMBER PART I, PRELIMINARY STATE, DECEMBER,
ELEMENTARY NURSING: CLASS B. 69%
24.3.44 BLUE STRIPES
1944 MARCH, MEDICINE: CLASS B, MAY, THEATRE LECTURES,
MAY PART II, PRELIMINARY STATE, OCTOBER GYNAECOLOGY: CLASS B,
DECEMBER, SURGERY: CLASS A
1945 JULY, HOSPITAL FINAL CLASS B, EXAMINATIONS QUALIFIED
FOR SILVER MEDAL, SEPTEMBER, FINAL STATE
SM MH ALVERSTOKE MH MV MH MV, 29 28 7.4 12 26.4 55.6 15.6H6

HOLIDAYS
1943 — 29TH JUNE 12 DAYS, 13TH OCTOBER 12 DAYS
1944 — 28TH FEBRUARY 2 WEEKS, 20 JULY 2 WEEKS
1945 — 1ST FEBRUARY 2 WEEKS, 10 SEPTEMBER 2 WEEKS,
       21ST DECEMBER 2 WEEKS
1946 — 26TH AUGUST 2 WEEKS
1948 — 16 FEB RE-ENTERED AS STAFF NURSE. N.
1949 — 21ST MAR SPECIAL LEAVE

ALVERSTOKE HOSPITAL, GOSPORT PO12 2AA, PRE 1948 — MILITARY,
GENERAL, POST 1948 — PRIVATE MILITARY, ACUTE

FORESTERHILL, ABERDEEN AB9 2ZB, FOUNDATION YEAR — 1739
PRE 1948 — LOCAL AUTHORITY, GENERAL, POST 1948 — NHS, ACUTE

THE MIDDLESEX HOSPITAL, MORTIMER STREET LONDON W1N 8AA
FOUNDATION YEAR — 1745, PRE 1948 — VOLUNTARY, GENERAL,
CANCER, POST 1948 — NHS, ACUTE

MOUNT VERNON HOSPITAL, NORTHWOOD HA6 2RN, FOUNDATION YEAR
— 1860, CONSUMPTION & DISEASES OF THE CHEST, PRE 1948
— VOLUNTARY, CHEST & CANCER, POST 1948 — NHS, ACUTE

STOKE MANDEVILLE HOSPITAL, AYLESBURY HP20 8AL, FOUNDATION
YEAR — C1900, FIRST BUILT AS AN ISOLATION HOSPITAL ACQUIRED
AS EMERGENCY HOSPITAL BY WAR OFFICE IN 1939, PRE 1948
— LOCAL AUTHORITY, 1942-1948 MINISTRY OF PENSIONS ISOLATION
& TUBERCULOSIS, POST 1948 — NHS, 1948-1951 MINISTRY
OF PENSIONS, ACUTE, ISOLATION & LONG STAY

THE MIDDLESEX HOSPITAL WARDS
ESSEX WYNTER — MOTHERS HELP, MATERNITY, MEYERSTEIN WING,
ROSALIND CHETWYND, WEBB JOHNSON & JOHN ASTOR, WEST WING, W3,
2ND FLOOR, 4TH FLOOR WOOLAVINGTON

MATRONS
MISS D M SMITH 1929, MISS M MARRIOTT 1946

SURGEONS
MR D H PATEY 1930, MR F W ROQUES 1930, MR I M JACKSON 1948

NURSING SISTERS
SISTER J BALL, SISTER BROWN — NIGHT SUPERINTENDENT,
SISTER EXLEY, SISTER GRANT, SISTER HAINES, S/JOHNSON, S/JOHNSTON,
S/PARKER, S/POTTER

NURSES
BERTWHISTLE, BUCKY, BRENDA HICKLEY (GLENDA), DYSON, FLOSSIE,
JORDAN, K. CAINE, PENNY, PERRY, MACKIE, MARDI, MARY, RUTH, SHAKE,
SLOGGETT, THORTON, RONALD (SURGEON) & VAL HUDSON, WESTON

VARIOUS STAFF
THE ADMIRAL, CHARLIE, DICKIE BIRD, FRANK DENNY — BARMAN,
LAURIE NATHAN, MR CULLEN — DENTAL

PATIENTS
DAVID DONALDSON, MR EASTON

COLLEAGUES/FRIENDS
ANN WARMSLEY, ANGLEFOR (SIC), ANGUS (GUS) MACKAY,
SAM & CECIL, JOHN — JOHN BOLTON, JOAN & FRED,
JOHNNY, PETER & COOKIE, KEVIN READ, MR JOHNSTONE,
STEWART (STEW) CHAMBERLAYNE

These pages contain all of the many names mentioned, either in a professional capacity as work colleagues or in friendship/acquaintances found in the diary.

The Hospital Wards, Staff & Colleagues

Mount Vernon Hospital wards
Hut 17, hut 20, hut 22

DOCTORS
Dr Janvrin

NURSING SISTERS
S/Morris, N/Sister Peake

NURSES
Bertwhistle, draper, mackie, margery, potter, rose, seymour, townsend, weston

VARIOUS STAFF/PATIENTS
Mr and mrs Mallory, reg, nance — patient
Seymour nurse/friend

Foresterhill Hospital wards
Isolation ante natal, greens x, labour ward maternity, Queens x, 1st floor maternity

DOCTORS
Dr Johnstone (mr)

NURSING SISTERS/STAFF NURSE
S/n milne, s/n cowis

NURSES
Assy Dickson, bertie, bigland, currance, duncan, giften, guiche, hope, isabelle, jenny, jenny wren, mac, mardi, marpery, morton, naryn, patience, perry, penny, reid, self, stables, stella

VARIOUS STAFF
Miss carter — lecturer

PATIENTS
Johnny boyce — 1st baby, george — baby

COLLEAGUES/FRIENDS
Mr johnston/mrs johnston, johnny, lester, wiebke

HISTORICAL AND SOCIAL EVENTS DURING 1946
Extracts taken from ~ *Chronology of British History,* Brockhampton Reference/Press.

Barbara Russell.
January 1st. 1946 - Somerset.

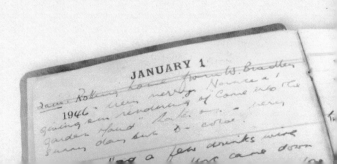

JANUARY 1
1946.

MONDAY 31 DECEMBER 1945

Tues 1   *2am. Rolling home from W. Bradley ~ very merry. Nance & I giving our rendering of 'Come into the Garden Maud'. Later on a very sunny day but D_ cold.*

Wed 2   *Unc went back to town. Very cold.*

Thurs 3   *Did my packing in the morning & then A. Lil & I sawed a large tree trunk up for Unc. Left the 'Close' about 3pm. Had a good journey, arrived here 8pm.*

Fri 4   *Have got quite a nice room warm at least! I am now on Essex Wynter as 'Mothers Help'. With S/Exley ~ hope I can stand the strain!*

Sat. 5   *Sister's weekend off! What fun. Mr Patey didn't turn up for his round fortunately! Everything went quite well.*

Sun 6   *Quite a peaceful day. Had the morning off.*

HISTORICAL AND SOCIAL EVENTS DURING 1946

3 JANUARY: EXECUTION OF WILLIAM JOYCE (LORD HAW HAW) FOR TREASON BY BROADCASTING NAZI PROPAGANDA FROM GERMANY

W. Bradley ~ West Bradley. The 'Close' ~ West End, Wedmore, Somerset.
'Come into the garden Maud' by Lord Alfred Tennyson.

Mon 7   Usual.

Tues 8   Had a letter from Bucky ~ she will be going out to Africa soon!

Wed 9   Evening off ~ went home. Everything much the same.

Thurs. 10   Had breakfast in bed & then went shopping. Walked to Mortlake in afternoon.

Fri 11   Usual.

Sat. 12   Had a long afternoon, went for a walk, then settled down to my book 'The Sunballs' (sic). Perry came to tea.

Sun 13   Had an afternoon. Finished reading my book. Had tea in my room. Tried to ring Bucky but both phones out of order.

Mon 14 *Had the evening off. Went to see 'The House on 92nd St.' Very good thriller. Slept at the hospital.*

Tues 15 *Had breakfast in bed then went to Bendicts with Perry. Had lunch at the hospital & then met Unc for tea & dinner. Went to pictures to see 'The Wicked Lady'. Not bad.*

Wed 16 *Had the morning off.*

Thurs. 17 *Had a long afternoon. Went to Odeon with Perry to see 'Caesar & Cleopatra'. Was rather disappointed. Had tea at Stewarts afterwards.*

Fri 18 *Usual. Sisters weekend off. Now for the fun! Poor Mr Easton died tonight.*

Sat. 19 *Mr Pateys round ~ everything went very well. Entertained him & Dyson & Shake to coffee afterwards in Sisters room! Had the evening off. Did some ironing also.*

---

* THE YEARS AFTER THE WAR SAW INTENSIVE DEVELOPMENT WITHIN THE INTERNATIONAL PHARMACEUTICAL INDUSTRY, INCLUDING THE INTRODUCTION OF PENICILLIN, MODERN VACCINES AND A HOST OF INNOVATIVE PRODUCTS

Bendicts ~ a local cafe/shop in London. **Stewarts** ~ a local tea room in London.

Sun 20 *Had an awful morning but rather funny. We had no maids at all ~ had all the washing up & the sweeping to do!*

Wed 23 *Usual. Expected Penny back but she didn't arrive.*

Thurs 24 *Went home in evening. Les & Peg are not getting married this year. A great pity ~ I think there is a lot of misunderstanding between them. Les is a queer chap ~ a bit like Father at times. Unfortunately we're all a bit like him now & then.*

Fri 25 *Had a very lazy day.*

Sun 27 *Usual. Had tea in my room ~ joined by Perry & Penny.*

Mon 28 *Had the evening off. Didn't go home. Went down to sitting room & wrote letters.*

Father

- THE NATIONAL HEALTH SERVICE ACT 1946 LED TO THE ESTABLISHMENT OF THE NATIONAL HEALTH SERVICE IN 1948
- THE NEW TOWNS ACT CREATED MAJOR NEW CENTRES OF POPULATION AND ALL NEEDED HEALTH SERVICES

Tues 29 *Penny brought my breakfast up. Had it in bed & then met Bucky at Bendicts for coffee & ices. Went shopping later & had tea with Penny. Met Unc & Mr Rushton for dinner in the evening.*

Wed 30 *Usual.*

Thurs 31 *Had a long afternoon. Went skating at Wembley Pk with Johnny & Peter & Cookie. Had a wonderful time. Sister goes off tonight for her long weekend. I hope we'll have a 'quiet weekend'.*

Fri 1 *Usual. Went out to coffee with Perry.*

Sat. 2 *Patey's round in the morning ~ everything went well. Had the afternoon off. Miserable weather ~ poured with rain.*

Sun 3 *Usual.*

Mon 4 *Evening off ~ went home ~ Peg was there.*

- THE ARTS COUNCIL OF GREAT BRITAIN (FORMERLY THE COUNCIL FOR THE ENCOURAGEMENT OF MUSIC AND THE ARTS, FOUNDED 1940) INCORPORATED

Wembley Pk ~ Wembley Park an area of northwest London, including Wembley Stadium.

Tues 5   *Got up quite early! Went up to Putney.*
Peg went back to Maidenhead.

Wed 6   *Penny is now on night duty. Casualty.*

Thurs. 7   *Went skating with Johnny. Nobody else came.*

Sat. 9   *Perry & Penny & I went out for coffee in the*
morning. The first time we have been off together for ages.

Sun 10   *Did some ironing & mending. Perry & I had tea*
in my room.

Mon 11   *Had the evening off. Washed my hair.*

Tues 12   *Had breakfast in bed. Did some shopping. Had tea*
at 'Tea Kettle' & then went to see 'Because of Him'. Very good.

Wed 13   *Usual.*

Thurs 14   *Perry & I both had 'longs' so we went to see*
'Saratoga Trunk'. Enjoyed it very much.

- THE FIRST ELECTRONIC COMPUTER, THE ENIAC
  (ELECTRONIC NUMERICAL INTEGRATOR AND CALCULATOR)
  WAS PUBLICLY DEMONSTRATED

Tea Kettle ~ a local cafe/shop in London.

Fri 15 *Sister off this evening. Had a wonderful time ~ 4 emergencies!*

Sat. 16 *Arrived on duty to find that Sister's chair had nearly gone up in smoke in the night. The whole side was burnt. Had to inform Matron!*

Sun 17 *Told by S/Potter at dinner time that Sister was off sick with flu! What a nice prospect.*

Tues 19 *Getting on quite well.*

Wed 20 *First teaching round that I've taken. Quite enjoyed it!*

Mon 25 *Sister back ~ very glad to see her. Nothing very terrible has happened though.*

Thurs. 28 *Mr Cullen dental H/s (sic) getting very cheeky! He's got a delightful accent! Can't understand a word!*

- PENGUIN CLASSICS LAUNCHED E.V.RIEU'S TRANSLATION OF 'THE ODYSSEY', MAKING CLASSIC TEXTS AVAILABLE TO EVERYONE
- NYLON STOCKINGS ARRIVE IN THE UK FROM THE USA FOR THE FIRST TIME

Queens ~ Ice Rink, Queensway, Bayswater, London.
The Strand ~ a London street, the hub of theatre and nightlife, three-quarters of a mile long.
Walter ~ family car, Les's first car.

Fri 1   *Went home in evening for weekend.*
Peg & Bill at home.

Sat. 2   *Got up early! Met Joyce & June at Queens,*
had a wonderful skate. Snowed in the aft.
Developed a b_ cold in evening.

Sun 3   *Felt lousy all day ~ couldn't be bothered to go*
back at night. I might get away with it!

Mon 4   *Arrived back at hosp. for 11am. Row in store!*
Sister was getting ready to come on duty! Put on innocent air
and it worked!

Sat. 9   *Went home in evening, after waiting about the*
Strand for an hour for Joan. Didn't go to Mary's show after all.

Sun 10   *Lovely day. Got up late. Went out for a ride on*
Walter in the aft. ~ goes beautifully. Did a lot of knitting.

---

1 MARCH: BANK OF ENGLAND NATIONALIZED

5 MARCH: THE TERM 'IRON CURTAIN' USED IN A SPEECH BY
SIR WINSTON CHURCHILL AT FULTON, MISSOURI, TO DESCRIBE
THE BARRIER DESCENDING ACROSS EUROPE

9 MARCH: THIRTY THREE FOOTBALL FANS CRUSHED
BY COLLASPED BARRIERS AT BURNDEN PARK IN BOLTON

Mon 11   *Usual. Had a long aft. Perry's brother arrived in London. She has 2 days off.*

Fri 15   *Sister starts her holiday today. Have been over to Webb Johnson ~ almost ready.*

Sat. 16   *Usual Sat. morning! The Admiral turned up as well. Have got 1/2 day today & tomorrow. Not a bad way to start!*

Sun 17   *Spent morning in bed. Spent afternoon getting advance guard of equipment moved over to W3.*

Mon 18   *Moved whole floor over to Webb Johnson & John Astor. What a job! Still I enjoyed organising it & getting it there. The boys helped a lot ~ including Charlie!*

Tues 19   *Have settled down now ~ just odds & ends. The new wards are really beautifully clean.*

Thurs 21   *Went skating.*

- PREMIERE OF 'A MATTER OF LIFE AND DEATH'
  BY MICHAEL POWELL AND EMERIC PRESSBURGER
- LORD WEBB JOHNSON DIED IN 1947, PRESIDENT
  OF R. C. OF SURGEONS, THE MIDDLESEX HOSPITAL

Albert Hall ~ the Royal Albert (concert) Hall, Kensington Gore, London.
Birbeck College ~ Birkbeck (part of the University of London) Malet Street, Bloomsbury.

Sat. 23 Usual.

Sun 24 Rather bored with life after whole weekend on!

Tues 26 Had 1/2 day. Went to pictures with Perry & then went to Albert Hall with Joyce & June.

Wed 27 Mary starts her holiday today.

Thurs. 28 Went skating. Met Margery & Doreen there.

Fri 29 Had the weekend ~ Went to Birbeck (sic) College to see Mary's 3 Foundation plays. Quite enjoyed them.

Sat. 30 Went down to see Boat Race in morning with Peg & A. Blanche & Mother. Cambridge lost by 3 lengths. Took bus to Kingston in afternoon with Jean & Peg.

Sun 31 Messed about. Went for walk along tow path in afternoon with Jean & Bill.

Mother

Les, Peg, Jean & Bill along the tow path. The Watermans Arms, Watneys Ales, Reids Stout

30 MARCH: THE BOAT RACE, OXFORD WON, CAMBRIDGE LOST

An annual boat race between Oxford and Cambridge University Boat Clubs, the championship course is 4 miles, 374 yards (6.8km) between Putney and Mortlake.

Mon 1   Had breakfast in bed & then arrived back here
at 12 m/d.

Tues 2   Had a busy morning. Wrote some letters
in the evening.

Fri 12   I've got a cold coming ~ & its my w/k off damn
it! Caught 6.40 from Paddington & arrived Maidenhead 8pm.

Sat. 13   Developed an awful cold. Took some ephedrine.
What bad luck! Did some gardening but b_ awful.

Sun 14   Cold a bit better. Rolled the turf in the morning,
had lunch & then lazed in the sun. Clare & little Angela come
in aft.

Mon 15   Caught 10.30 train from Maidenhead. On duty
12 m/d.

Wed 17   Took the morning off & went out with Mary
& Perry to Ma-S (sic). Had a good tuck in!

---

2 APRIL: THE ROYAL MILITARY ACADEMY AT SANDHURST CREATED
21 APRIL: THE DEATH OF THE ECONOMIST JOHN MAYNARD KEYNES
• EXECUTION BY HANGING OF NEVILLE HEATH FOR MURDER

Paddington ~ Paddington Station, the London terminus of the Great Western Railway.
Ephedrine ~ for cold remedies, relaxing the airways and making breathing easier.
Ma-S (sic) ~ unknown.

Thurs 18 *Usual. Met Reg in evening. Went to see 'Lady Windermeres Fan' in evening. He has to go back on Monday.*

Fri 19 *Had a 'cut throat' attempted suicide in at dinner time. Busy.*

Sat. 20 *Round as usual in morning. Had a busy time with emergencies etc. Had to put up Laurie Nathan!*

Sun 21 *Easter! And I have the weekend on. A glorious weekend too. Brenda Hickley (awful girl) arrived in Sw from Obs.*

Mon 22 *Easter Monday. Had this evening. Mother rang up ~ worried because she thought I was going home last Fri! Messed about in evening. Better go home tomorrow.*

Tues 23 *Went home in afternoon. Mother had gone to the pictures. Back here in the evening.*

Wed 24 *Usual.*

Sw from Obs ~ South Wing or Seymour Ward from Obstetrics.

Fri 26 W/k ~ went home in the evening. Mother has gone down to Maidenhead. Just Jean, Bill, Les & myself.

Sat. 27 Usual. Went up to Putney in morning.

Sun 28 Messed about.

Mon 29 On duty 12 md.

Wed 1 Met Perry & Penny & went out to coffee. Had a long talk.

Fri 3 W/k on.

Sun 5 Spent the weekend 'tidying up' for Sister.

Mon 6 Took 1/2 day today. Don't suppose I'd get it tomorrow. Mary and I went to Dickins & Jones for tea ~ had a wonderful tea!. Washed my hair in evening.

Tues 7 Sister Exley back this morning.

- DR BENJAMIN SPOCK PUBLISHES BABY AND CHILD CARE. SPARKING A CHILD-REARING REVOLUTION
- BRITISH PROTECTORATE OF JORDAN ENDED AND IT BECAME AN INDEPENDENT KINGDOM

Dickins & Jones ~ a high-quality department store in Regent Street, London.

Wed 8 Busy.

Thurs 9 Went skating in evening with Joyce & met the rest of the crowd.

Fri 10 Busy day off. Went rowing with Mary on Serpentine in morning ~ had a wonderful time. Coffee at Green Lizard before & an ice in Park afterwards. Met Joyce in evening & went to flicks.

Sat 11 Usual. Had evening off ~ got off at 6.45pm. Felt very tired.

Sun 12 Terribly busy on the wards. Short of staff & fed up! Went down about my holiday ~ have fixed it for 24 Aug. after a struggle!

Mon 13 Sister back this morning after a hectic weekend. I have evening & d/o. Went out for walk in evening. Then went to pictures.

• NEW BODLEIAN LIBRARY OPENED

Flicks/pictures ~ cinema.
Serpentine ~ once, one of the best lakes for skating was in Hyde Park.
Green Lizard ~ local cafe/shop near the Serpentine.

MAY/JUNE 1946

Thurs. 23 Went skating in evening with Joyce. I am going
to Northwood on 15th of June. I'm not surprised.

Sat. 25 Sister off.

Sun 26 Sister off.

Thurs 30 Busy.

Fri 31 Couldn't have evening as Sister has 1/2 d. Have
got the w/k off. Felt ready for it too.

Sat. 1 Joyce couldn't come skating so stayed in bed.
Went home in aft. Fitted for my Bridesmaids' frock.

Sun 2 Messy day. Rained & then the sun shone
alternately all day. Joan & Fred came over in aft. Cycled up
to Hosp in evening & then came back to sleep.

Mon 3 Peggy brought me breakfast in bed. Got up 10.30.
Had coffee with Peg & then came up to Hosp. Went out with

---

1 JUNE: INTRODUCTION OF TELEVISION LICENCES IN BRITAIN

Aldwych Corner ~ local cafe/shop in London.
Derby ~ taking place each year in June at Epsom Downs, the Epsom Derby
is a prestigious flat, thoroughbred horse race.
Westminster Br. ~ display ends with the firing of 50 magnesium shells
and the playing of the National Anthem.

Mary in aft. Had tea at Aldwych Corner. Saw 'Spellbound'
with Joyce in evening.

Tues 4   Had morning off.

Wed 5   Had 1/- on Radiotherapy in the Derby but he
came 4th or 5th. Airborne won. Had a long aft. Went shopping,
then had tea in my room.

Thurs 6   Anniversary of D-day.

Sat. 8   'V DAY'. Watched bits of the procession from Hosp.
roof with binoculars. Poured with rain in aft so couldn't go out.
Perry & I made our way to Westminster Br. in evening plus
thousands of other people with the same idea. Managed to get
onto bridge & had a wonderful view of barges lit up & fire-
works. Back at 1.30pm.

Tues 11   Usual. Went to pictures in evening with Mary.
Poured with rain.

---

5 JUNE: DERBY DAY

6 JUNE: 'D' DAY ANNIVERSARY

8 JUNE: 'VE' DAY ANNIVERSARY PROCESSION

D-day ~ The D-Day allied landings on the beaches of Normandy in northern France
at the start of a major offensive against the Germans.

'V' Day ~ Victory in Europe, Germany surrenders.

Wed 12 *Had day off with Mary. Went to Bendicts in morning. Had lunch & then did some shopping. Brought a suitcase (Jean's & Bill's present). Went to pictures in evening. Then went round the illuminations. Wonderful sight.*

Thurs. 13 *Usual day. Met Unc in evening & went down the river from Westminster to Tower Br. on a steamer. Wonderful sight.*

Fri 14 *Last day on Webb J & J Astor. All very sorry to leave. The chief trouble is Charlie but I can't get over that, if I want to.*

Sat. 15 *Got up 9am & finished packing, then caught 10.15 train to Northwood. Arrived on duty 12 m/d Hut 20 ~ S/Morris. Not very busy in comparison to Webb J. I am going to have alternate wk's with Sister, which is very nice.*

14 JUNE: DEATH OF JOHN LOGIE BAIRD IN BEXHILL-ON-SEA, SUSSEX. SCOTTISH ENGINEER AND PIONEER OF THE FIRST WORKING TELEVISION

Trafalgar Square fountain at night

Illuminations ~ from 10pm until midnight, up to Saturday 15th June around London.
Westminster to Tower Br. on a steamer ~ to view the illuminations and floodlit cruisers.

Sun 16 *Have got a cubicle to myself & have had great fun arranging it, off in the aft. Wrote some letters & had tea in my room.*

Wed 19 *Went up to town & met Mary. Went to Royal & saw 'The Common Touch' & 'Come Live with Me'. Had supper & then caught Green Line coach back.*

Sat. 22 *Sister w/k off.*

Wed 26 *Mary came down here. Went for a walk & then ended up at Northwood Hills for wonderful supper & pictures. Saw 'Dragonwyck'. Quite good.*

Fri 28 *Evening off. Went home.*

Sat. 29 *Messed about as usual.*

Sun 30 *Messed about in morning. Met Mary in aft & went to Hampton Court by the river. Took some tea etc. Back home in evening. Took Green Line from Park Lane all the way here.*

- THE SCHOOL MILK ACT PROVIDES A FREE THIRD OF A PINT OF MILK TO ALL SCHOOL CHILDREN

Green Line coach ~ services as at May 1946, immediately after their full reinstatement following wartime curtailment.

Green Line from Park Lane ~ Green Line services resumed after the war in February 1946.

JULY 1946

Wed 3 *Had evening off. Had a cycle ride & then went to Northwood Hills to see 'Bedelia'. Quite good.*

Fri 5 *Sisters w/k off.*

Wed 10 *Usual. Sat in the sun!*

Thurs 11 *Still hot. Lazed outside & slept out all night. Wonderful feeling. Rose & Townsend did the same.*

Fri 12 *Off duty at 5pm. Went home.*

Sat. 13 *Got up fairly early. Went up to Apollo theatre & booked seats for Aug. 6th for Grand National Night. Should be good. Went swimming at Roehampton in aft.*

Sun 14 *Had breakfast in bed. Drove down to Maidenhead in aft. Quite a nice day, although cool. Had tea, picked some raspberries. Then had supper & had a wonderful drive home. Arrived back at M.V.H at 12 midnight.*

Mon 15 *Usual. Cleaned bike in aft. & mended puncture.*

Tues 16 *Depressing day! Poured with rain all morning. Had a LA (sic) & wrote some letters. Had tea in my room & finished reading Wuthering Heights.*

Fri 26 *W/K off. Went to stay with A. Blanche. Nearly got flooded out. Terrific cloudburst just before I left.*

Sat. 27 *Had breakfast in bed. Walked up to Clapham Common in morning. Had tea out in the garden. Went to Wimbledon Theatre in evening & saw 'The Elusive Lady' with Mark Houston & Evelyn Laye.*

Sun 28 *Had breakfast in bed again! Cut the grass & dug up potatoes. Went to pictures in evening.*

Mon 29 *Arrived back at M.V.H. 10.30.*

Aunt Blanche

6 JULY: FORMATION OF YOUNG CONSERVATIVES

22 JULY: KING DAVID HOTEL, BRITISH MILITARY HQ IN JERUSALEM, BOMBED BY JEWISH TERRORISTS

22 JULY: INTRODUCTION OF BREAD RATIONING

Roehampton ~ swimming pool & lido, Laverstoke Gardens, off Danebury Avenue, Roehampton, London.

'Wuthering Heights' ~ Emily Jane Brontë's only novel.

Thurs. 1 S/Morris off on holiday.

Sun 4 Usual.

Mon 5 Went home in evening. Called at Nurses Home for some of my things. Mother & Les down at Maidenhead.

Tues 6 Got up quite early. Penny rang me up in the morning. Went out shopping. Bought wedding present for Jean & Bill. Met Mother & bought a trunk & then had tea. Joyce, Mary & I went to see Leslie Banks in 'Grand National Night' at Apollo. Very good indeed. Had chop suey afterwards.

Wed 7 Usual.

Thurs 8 Had 1/2 day. Went to Aylesbury to see Penny. Had tea at the Bell & talked. Came back to Northwood & went to pictures. Saw 'I see a Dark Stranger' ~ very good. Had to cycle back in dark ~ forgot my lamp.

Fri 9 Usual.

---

6 **AUGUST:** 'GRAND NATIONAL NIGHT' APOLLO
    THEATRE/LESLIE BACHS
• **FIRST MEETING OF THE**
    UNITED NATIONS
    ORGANISATION

The Bell ~ The Green, Aylesbury, Buckinghamshire.

Many Happy Returns of the
Day. August 6th 1946.
with love from Nance

Sat. **10** *Had aft. on call. Wrote some letters. Awful aft. poured with rain. But lovely evening.*

Sun **11** *Drank coffee nearly all the morning. Had aft. off. Wrote to Aunt Lil & Unc.*

Fri **23** *Left ward at 4.30 but taxi didn't turn (sic). Dr. Janvrin gave me a lift down to St. Just managed to get train. Arrived Paddington well on time. Case very heavy! Met Unc at Westbury. A. Lil, Nance & Pooh at Wells as usual.*

Sat. **24** *Nance has changed for the worst since I was here before. I don't know what has come over her.*

Sun **25** *Went over to W. Bradley as usual. Nice to see them all again. Went out for walk & then played cards. I lost!*

Tues **27** *Rain!*

Wed **28** *Extracted the honey with Unc. Very sticky business!*

---

13 AUGUST: THE DEATH OF H. G. WELLS

- FILM DIRECTOR, MURIEL BOX, WINS A BEST
  SCREENPLAY OSCAR FOR HER FILM
  THE SEVENTH VEIL

Pooh ~ Black labrador dog, family pet.

Thurs. 29 *Picked some stuff for A. Lil to take into market.*

Fri 30 *Still raining! Went into Wells with A. Lil. A. Kate came back with us, stayed to tea. A. Lil & I drove her back after tea.*

Sat. 31 *Messed about in house. Bottled the honey ~ 29½lbs.*

Sun 1 *Went over to West Bradley in afternoon. Unc & I went mushrooming as usual. Played cards in evening! Lost as usual!*

Mon 2 *Went to Bath in the car for the day. Lovely day ~ didn't rain until we were coming back. Nance & A. Lil bought new hats for the wedding.*

Tues 3 *Left Wedmore 8.30am. Caught train & dropped off at Reading. Unc & I went out to Sonning to look at house ~ no good. Poured with rain most of time. Arrived home about 7pm.*

Wed 4 *Had a Busy Day. Jean packing, Peg & I doing 'last minute jobs before wedding'.*

- CEYLON GAINED INDEPENDENCE
- THE ORGANIC FARMING PIONEER, LADY EVE BALFOUR FOUNDS THE SOIL ASSOCIATION

Victoria ~ Victoria Station, providing train services to the Kent coast, Medway towns and routes to Sussex.
Bognor ~ Bognor Regis in West Sussex for convalescence.
Wigmore St. ~ City of Westminster, London.

Thurs 5 Jean's Wedding day! Great excitement in morning. Went up by car to fetch flowers from Wigmore St. Sun shone beautifully. Everything went very well. I got rather tight towards end! Sent Jean & Bill off with plenty of confetti. Nance & I went out in the evening.

Fri 6 Nance & I went up to Putney. Had some coffee. Had tea out & went to pictures. Saw 'Captive Heart' & 'Mr. Ace'. Good programme.

Sat. 7 Saw Nance off at Victoria to Bognor. Mother also went off to A. Blanche for w/k. Peg came up tea time. Peter came round in evening with snaps. Very good indeed.

Sun 8 Messed about. Horrible day ~ poured with rain. Peter came round with photos just before I left. Has done some very nice enlargements.

Mon 9 Finished unpacking.

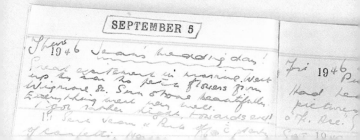

SEPTEMBER 5

Tues 10 *Had evening, went skating at Queens.*
Met Joyce & Margery there, also Potter. Had a good skate.

Wed 11 *Had 1/2 day. Took my bike to Northwood Hills*
to be repaired. Had tea at Ricky & went to pictures.

Thurs 12 *Nice day again. Did some washing in afternoon,*
& worked out bus route for tomorrow. Shall travel by 6 buses!

Fri 4 *Went home in evening.*

Sat. 5 *Met Joyce in morning, did some shopping.*
Went to see 'Overlanders' an Australian film ~ very good
indeed. Had tea with her & then went to Ice Hockey at Wembley.

Sun 6 *Had a celebration for Les' birthday. Jean & Bill*
& Peg & Peter came over. Also A.B. Had a birthday cake!

Mon 7 *Les' birthday. Back to Northwood in morning.*

- THE ROYAL COMMISSION ON EQUAL PAY RECOMMENDS
  TEACHERS, LOCAL GOVERNMENT OFFICERS AND CIVIL
  SERVANTS SHOULD ALL RECEIVE EQUAL PAY

Queens ~ Ice Rink, Queensway, Bayswater, London.
Ricky ~ Rickmansworth near to Northwood Hills.
Ice Hockey at Wembley ~ during the 1940s, 50s and 60s the arena was
used by the Wembley Lions and the Wembley Monarchs, two ice hockey teams.

Tues 15   *Nance arrived from Somerset plus Unc & A. Lil in car. Has gone to Hut 17. Looks pretty ill. Went into see her in the evening. Draper leaves today.*

Wed 16   *Usual. I suppose I shall take over Hut 22.*

Thurs 17   *Went home in evening after skating.*

Fri 18   *Mother went up to Hosp. To go in about 14 days time. Met Penny afterwards & had good talk & coffee. Home in aft. Went to pictures with June and Joyce in evening. Saw 'Theirs is the Glory'.*

Sat. 19   *Usual.*

Sun 20   *Usual.*

Mon 21   *Mary was coming down here but she had her off duty changed. Messed about instead.*

---

7 OCTOBER: THE RADIO PROGRAMME 'WOMANS HOUR' PRESENTED BY ALAN IVIESON, WAS LAUNCHED AT 2PM EVERY AFTERNOON. THE NEWSPAPER CRITICS: 'DANGEROUSLY RADICAL' AND 'LAUGHABLY OBSESSED WITH DOMESTIC DETAIL'

16 OCTOBER: WAR CRIMES TRIBUNAL, WORLD WAR II, AT NUREMBERG ENDED; EXECUTIONS CARRIED OUT

Tues 22 Had aft ~ went down to Northwood & changed library books.

Wed 23 Had a 1/2 day but all my arrangements fell through. Mary had a morning & Joyce couldn't come skating. Went to pictures & had tea at Tea Kettle. Saw 'Black Beauty' & 'Stanley & Livingstone'. Both very good.

Thurs 24 Went to see Nance in aft. Then had tea in my room. B_ cold day. Have worn my pullover under uniform. What will it be like in winter!

Wed 6 Had 1/2 day. Went up to Middlesex, met Perry, but too late for tea. Then went skating. My boots still being mended so had to hire a pair. Couldn't get on at all well.

Fri 8 Home in the evening. Mother goes into Putney Hosp. Sunday evening.

Sat. 9 Went up to town & booked seats for ballet at

- **9 NOVEMBER: LORDS MAYOR SHOW**
- DAME ALIX KILROY BECOMES MOST SENIOR WOMAN CIVIL SERVANT WHEN APPOINTED UNDER-SECRETARY TO THE BOARD OF TRADE
- MARRIAGE BAR IS ABOLISHED IN THE POST OFFICE/CIVIL SERVICE

OCTOBER 23

OCTOBER 24

Covent Garden. Then went along to see 'Lord Mayors Show'
~ quite good. Home for tea. A. Blanche came in the evening.

Sun 10 A. Blanche brought up tea in bed. I went over
to Jean & Bill's about 12. Had dinner & sat round fire.
Then had tea! Played bridge in evening. They have got a very
nice place there. Stayed the night ~ in a large brass bed.

Mon 11 Arrived back here ~ on duty 11am. Very busy
now. Saw Nance in the evening. Rang up Les ~ Mother O.K
but it was a growth? malignant. Not a pleasant prospect.
Can only hope for the best.

Tues 12 Went skating in the evening. Had my own skates
back & got on very much better.

Wed 13 Had a busy day. Saw Nance in the afternoon &
mended some stockings. Meant to do lots more but didn't have
time. Unc came down in the evening and brought a melon!

Tues 31 Had a party (farewell!) with Mackie, Weston
& Bertwhistle. Weston got drunk & I had to escort her to her
room. I had already had a few drinks with A. Lil to celebrate
her birthday. Our party was very merry ~ message from
N/sister via Peake to shut up! Afterwards I drank coffee with
A. Lil & she never guessed!

BARB & NANCE — DRESSING UP!

'The Aunts' from West Bradley.
With Aunt Win, Aunt Em, Unc,
Aunt Lil, Barbara and Pooh

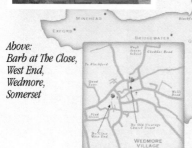

Above:
Barb at The Close,
West End,
Wedmore,
Somerset

WEDMORE, SOMERSET
THE CLOSE & THE OLD VICARAGE

"Jean's Wedding day! Great excitement in morning. Went up by car to fetch flowers from Wigmore St. Sun shone beautifully."

'60 years a Queen' (a book published on the anniversary of Queen Victoria's 60th reigning year). Jean and Les (gave Jean away). Peg & Barbara

Barbara, Stan, Bill, Susan/Angela, Jean, Peg

59

HISTORICAL AND SOCIAL EVENTS DURING 1947
Extracts taken from ~ *Chronology of British History*, Brockhampton Reference/Press.

60

HISTORICAL AND SOCIAL EVENTS DURING 1947

- THE KING AND QUEEN WENT TO SOUTH AFRICA, TAKING THE TWO PRINCESSES, ELIZABETH AND MARGARET WITH THEM. ELIZABETH CELEBRATED HER 21ST WHILST THERE
- THE DIARY OF ANNE FRANK IS FIRST PUBLISHED IN THE NETHERLANDS

Wed 1 *Had a few drinks with Nance & A. Lil. Unc came down in evening. Also Seymour came along. Had some Christmas cake.*

Sat. 11 *Packing! Came up to town & met Reg, Les & girlfriend. Went to Frascati's for dinner & dance. Reg going back to Germany tomorrow.*

Sun 12 *Last day at Middlesex & Northwood! Had the aft off ~ Les & Peg came down in car to collect my luggage. Took them across to see Nance. Spent the evening with Nance.*

Mon 3 *Frozen up.*

Tues 4 *Frozen up but thawed out.*

Wed 5 *Frozen up but thawed out again.*

Thurs. 6 *Still cold & icy.*

Fri 7 *Caught 12.30 train from Paddington & arrived*

---

1 **JANUARY:** BRITAINS COAL INDUSTRY NATIONALIZED

M. Hole. The Close. Wedmore. Somerset. Febi 1947.

Wells 4.17. Aunt Lil met me with car. Not much snow here.

Sat. 8 *Started to snow in afternoon & went on steadily all evening.*

Sun 9 *Snow very deep. Unc & I put chains on the car but they didn't fit well & we had to turn back & didn't go to W. Bradley.*

Mon 10 *Went to W. Bradley for tea. Aunts just the same as ever! Played cards. Roads quite clear.*

Tues 11 *Tried to take Unc to Frome but roads too icy. Had to turn back & go via Wells.*

Wed 12 *Went into Weston Super Mare in the car with Aunt Lil. Roads not too bad.*

Thurs 13 *Jeans birthday.*

Sat. 15 *Usual.*

---

12 FEBRUARY: CHRISTIAN DIOR LAUNCHES HIS 'NEW LOOK' FOR WOMEN

Frascati's ~ Italian restaurant/Oxford Street, London.

Sun 16 *Went over to W. Bradley & saw the kittens. Played cards as usual. Rang Les up to find out whether Mother had gone. She arrived quite safely. Jean & Bill back at 5pm.*

Mon 17 *Had a wonderful bonfire in orchard of all small stuff. Have practically cleared orchard. Aunt Lil & Unc sawing.*

Tues 18 *The 'Lumber Camp' again. Had wonderful bonfire again in orchard.*

Wed 19 *Continued 'logging' in the morning & had bonfire. Caught aft. train from Wells & arrived London 8pm.*

Thurs 20 *Went up to Kings X Station about my ticket & sleeping berth. Arranged it all. Snow again.*

Fri 21 *Did some washing & ironing.*

Sat. 22 *Started packing. Went skating on the Serpentine with Joyce. Quite good but too much snow. Did some slides.*

---

20 FEBRUARY: LORD MOUNTBATTEN APPOINTED LAST VICEROY OF INDIA TO OVERSEE THE TRANSFER OF POWER TO THE INDEPENDENT GOVERNMENTS OF INDIA AND PAKISTAN

- INDEPENDENCE GRANTED TO INDIA AND BRITISH ASIAN COLONIES, THE INDIAN EMPIRE CAME TO AN END

Sun 23 Jean & Bill went down to Eastbourne by car to fetch Mother. She has had a very good time, looks much better, & is going to stay a few days with Jean.

Mon 24 Finished packing & sent luggage off to Aberdeen.

Tues 25 Went down to see Nance in afternoon. She was not looking too well, had some nasty styes on her eyes. Unc came down in evening.

Wed 26 Went over to Jean's in the aft. Had tea & stayed the evening.

Thurs 27 Mother came back with Jean & Bill in car. Looking very well. Played cards in evening.

Fri 28 Met Mary in the morning for coffee. Went back to home with her. Finished packing in aft. Had tea & caught 7.30pm train from Kings X. Had a sleeper & slept very well! Woke up once at Newcastle.

- MARIA CALLAS MAKES HER FIRST APPEARANCE IN A PERFORMANCE OF LA GIOCANDA BY PONCHIELLI

Lumber Camp ~ work party to clear small orchard at The Close.
Serpentine ~ once, one of the best lakes for skating in Hyde Park.
Kings X Station, Kings X ~ King's Cross Station, is the London terminus for the east coast main line.

Sat. 1   *Awoke when we arrived at Edinburgh. Had tea & biscuits. Could see sea from windows, also lots of snow. Sun shining. Arrived Aberdeen 3 hrs late. Came up to Hosp. by bus. Have very nice room.*

Sun 2   *On duty in isolation Ante Natal. Not very busy. Went out in snow in the morning. Took some photographs.*

Mon 3   *Had day off but had medical exam & lecture in morning. Finished by 11am. Went down to town & had lunch there. Came back & washed hair & wrote letters. Went back to Aberdeen for tea & pictures. Saw 'School for Secrets'.*

Tues 4   *Had morning off. Wrote letters. 1st proper lecture by Miss Carter in evening. Awfully funny! I'm sure I shall laugh one of these days.*

Sun 16   *Moved to Labour Ward. I think I shall like it very much.*

- CHINA GIVES VOTES TO WOMEN

Fri 21 *Delivered 1st baby ~ Johnny Boyce ~ no tears?*
Had evening off.

Sat. 22 *Had day off. Had breakfast in bed & then went
to Bridge of Don & walked down to sea. Also collected photos
~ very good. Went skating in evening.*

Mon 24 *Penny had day off.*

Tues 25 *Penny & I both had evening ~ had coffee & went
to pictures.*

Wed 26 *Had an evening. Went out for walk & ended up
at pictures.*

Thurs 27 *Delivered 2nd baby today, another boy.
No tears! Also bought Biro pen. Middlesex Hosp. badge arrived
~ very nice.*

Fri 28 *Very busy day on Labour ward ~ Had 3 Caesars
& 1 at night.*

- CICELY LUDLAM BECOMES THE FIRST OFFICIAL BRITISH
  WOMAN DIPLOMAT WITH HER POSTING TO BELGRADE
  AS THIRD SECRETARY (COMMERCIAL)

3 Caesars ~ A caesarean section, an operation to deliver a baby.

Sat. 29 *Had 1/2 day ~ awfully misty day. Couldn't go to the sea. Went down to Aberdeen for tea, & lost ivory brooch when running for bus. Went back but it was broken. Cambridge won the boat race!*

Sat. 5 *Had day off. As usual poured with rain. Transferred myself to Queens X. Seems very nice? First impressions!*

Wed 16 *Mother's birthday.*

Thurs. 17 *Evening off. Went to see students show 'Cakes & Ale'. Enjoyed it very much.*

Fri 18 *Had early breakfast then took bus to Balmoral. Hourly ride. Walked right into grounds & into Castle as the painters had gone to lunch & left the door open! Then went to Braemars.*

Sat. 19 *Students torchlight procession.*

29 MARCH: BOAT RACE, CAMBRIDGE WON – OXFORD LOST

1 APRIL: RAISING OF SCHOOL LEAVING AGE TO 15

Students torchlight procession ~ established in 1889 by nurses of the Royal Infirmary who used to run the Torcher Parade to help fund the wards.

Thurs. 1   Had evening off. Went to pictures.

Fri 2   Cycled to Loch Skene in afternoon. Had a wonderful ride. Took some photos. Had to come back early for lecture.

Sun 4   Went on night duty. Moved up to Attic. Jenny Wren bit of a drip! In my hair all day & night too!

Tues 13   Builders started upstairs. Couldn't sleep, so moved downstairs. Now have room to myself, thank goodness.

Thurs 15   Had night off. Met Penny at 10.30 & went for hike along coast to Cove. Took our lunch. Lovely day. Arrived back very tired. Went to pictures in evening.

Fri 16   Had wonderful 'lie in', had breakfast in bed. Got up for lunch & lazed in garden. Met Penny & Dr. Johnstone for tea at Fullers. Quite a nice lad. Went up to Hazlehead afterwards. On duty at night.

•   FOUNDATION OF ST BENETS HALL OXFORD

Fullers ~ a local tea rooms/shop in Aberdeen.

Sat. 17 *Went up to Hosp. for Ward Round. Penny is selling flags ~ for unmarried Mothers & Babies! Came home & had some tea then went to bed.*

Sun 18 *Stella back from holiday ~ Currance has 6 nights off ~ Stella on with me. Wonderful night.*

Mon 19 *Had a crash on my bike. Grazed my knee & elbow (same one again!)*

Tues 20 *Lovely day. Lay in sun on lawn in morning. Up to Mat. for lecture.*

Wed 21 *Great night.*

Fri 30 *Had night off, also Penny. Cycled to Echt & surrounding country ~ Hill of Fare. Had lunch & tea out, but poured with rain coming back. Got soaked. Had to give Penny a dress & cardigan of mine!*

- GROUNDNUT SCHEME IN TANGANYIKA BEGAN

Erilea (sic) 1947

Sat. 31   Met Dr. Johnstone for tea & went to Hazlehead afterwards. He seems quite nice but rather shy. Not as jolly as Johnny. Going back to Mat. Penny coming down to Q.X.

Sun 1   Arrived back at Foresterhill, worst luck. N/D Ante Natal. Not bad. But nothing like Queens X.

Sat. 7   Last night in Ante Natal.

Sun 8   Started 1st floor with Giften. Not very interesting! Had supper at Q.X.

Sat. 14   Caught 9am Bus out to Inverurie, & met by Mr. Johnston. Very nice man. Both talk an awful lot. Have to work hard to keep one's end up! 3 lovely cocker spaniels & 2 pups. Stayed up all day & had wonderful night in bed.

Sun 15   Had breakfast in bed & then got up about 12.30 pm! Back here for duty & night. Brought back some flowers for my room.

- NORTH CHANNEL BETWEEN NORTHERN IRELAND AND SCOTLAND FIRST SWUM BY TOM BLOWER OF NOTTINGHAM

Sat. 21 *Last night on night duty. Must say I shall be glad to come off. Have not enjoyed N/D here at Foresterhill.*

Sun 22 *Met Penny & her Mother & Father at Hotel & went out in car in afternoon. Had tea by Deeside & then back again about 7.30pm. Had tea & sandwiches & then drove me back here about 10pm.*

Mon 23 *Started Day Duty on isolation. Much the same as before!*

Fri. 27 *Had evening off. Went to see 'California', with Stella & Penny. Thoroughly enjoyed it.*

Sat. 28 *Had Test in morning. Not too bad. Caught 1pm bus out to Inverurie but got off at Kintore instead. Luckily man from Glasgow gave me a lift. Showed them the photos. Came back in evening & went to Ballet (Swan Lake).*

- FIRST BRITISH NUCLEAR REACTOR
  BUILT AT HARWELL

*Nance in bathchair,
June 1947 MVH,
Mount Vernon Hospital*

Tues 1 *Had evening off. Penny & I went to see Alastair Sim in 'Dr Angelus' at His Majesty's. Very good indeed.*

Wed 2 *Had 1/2 day but weather not good, so only messed about. Went to pictures in evening. R. Newton in 'Temptation Harbour'. Quite good.*

Thurs 3 *Had some worrying news from home ~ Mother getting worse. Went skating in evening to try & shake off depression. Didn't succeed.*

Fri 4 *Had lecture this morning. Finished 2nd matinee coat for Jean's infant. Pressed it in the evening & put in ribbons. Looks very nice.*

Mon 7 *Had a letter from Les, Mother's condition worse & due to fresh growth. Only a matter of a few months. I can hardly believe it, & yet have been half expecting it for sometime. Have felt utterly miserable all day.*

- FIRST TURBOPROP ENGINE IN USE (IN THE ROLLS ROYCE DART)

Matinee coat ~ hand knitted outer coat/cardigan for a baby.

Tues 8   *Had a short note from Jean to say that Auntie Wyn died early yesterday. I'm wondering now what else will happen.*

Wed 9   *Had day off. Lecture in morning. Letter from Peg. Replied same day. Penny & I went to pictures & afterwards to Carnival on beach. Enjoyed the 'Dodge-ems' very much. Felt better afterwards. Managed to forget for a little while.*

Thurs 10   *Off in afternoon. Lecture in evening. Still feeling pretty miserable. Wrote to Middlesex Hosp. for staff job & Gen. Nurse Council for information about Switzerland.*

Fri 11   *Had evening off. Did some swotting & then wrote to Mother.*

Sat. 12   *Went down to Queens X. for supper party ~ rather a queer one, Jenny & Assy Dickson ~ Bigland & Reid, Penny & I & Mac. A pity Stella or Marpery wasn't there. Nobody knew what to say to the other. S/N Cowis also came & helped a lot. Nice girl.*

- GATT (GENERAL AGREEMENT ON TARIFFS AND TRADE)
  SIGNED BY 23 NATIONS

Carnival ~ the Aberdeen Fun Beach had a permanent fun fair, indoor sports and leisure area, lying just to the north of Aberdeen and was purchased by the council in 1947.
Gen. Nurse Council ~ for England and Wales, in 1947, offices at 23, Portland Place, London.

Sun 13   *Penny back up here at Maty. ~ on Ante Natal.*
I started on 1st floor. Awful routine. Had evening off. An hour
on the roof ~ did some ironing etc.

Mon 14   *Penny went up to London for her brothers wedding.*

Tues 15   *Les wrote to say Mother much worse. I decided*
to go home ~ saw Miss Carter ~ arranged to leave on 6.8.
Did not sleep much. Mother died 10pm this evening.

Wed 16   *Arrived on time Kings Cross but was too late*
to see Mother. Jean & Bill both there. Had arrangements
to see to. Jean & Bill went back home.

Thurs. 17   *Had a 'lay in', as I felt very tired. Can't seem*
to believe it yet. Peg came up ~ very good to see her.

Fri 18   *Ordered wreaths.*

Sun 20   *Went over to see Jean & Bill. Jean had started*
vague pains, but very cheerful. Left about 10pm.

Queens X. ~ ward at Foresterhill Hospital.
Maty. ~ Maternity on Ante Natal.
1st floor ~ Nursery ward at the Middlesex Hospital.

JULY 1947

Mon 21 Bill rang up to say that the baby was dead ~ very difficult delivery. Funeral at 2.30pm. Trying to arrange to put baby in same grave. Went over to see Jean ~ quite cheerful still but terribly disappointed.

Tues 22 Caught 10am train Kings Cross. Unc came to see me off. Have bought the Old Vicarage. Train held up few miles out of Stonehaven. Arrived here 12.30am. Penny met me, bless her!

Wed 23 Feeling rather flat & depressed, especially about the baby. Started on 1st floor but going to suit Nursery after all.

Thurs 24 Liking Nursery. But terribly sad & depressed. Suppose I'll get over it.

Mon 28 Have decided to carry on with Youth Hostel trip, & have written to all Youth Hostels on our route.

Wed 30 Aberdeen Shipping Co. say they have no vacancies for Sept. Looks as though we will have to go by train after all.

Old Vicarage ~ Church Street, Wedmore, Somerset.
Aberdeen Shipping Co. ~ in relation to a possible trip (originally for Sept 23 1947 but then undertaken in August 1948). The United Steamship Co Ltd, London & North Eastern Railway (LNER) and the Danish Tourist Bureau, promoting travel to Denmark, via sea routes between Harwich and Esbjerg.

Fri 1   Had evening & day off. Went out to Inverurie after lecture. Mardi was there, also Bertie, but he left so came back to Aberdeen. Showed them photographs.

Sat. 2   Had morning in bed, & then messed about generally. Machined sleeping bags & left again on 9.30pm bus. Brought back enormous amount of fruits.

Sun 3   Penny & I had strawberries & raspberries & cream, also Morton, nearly made ourselves sick!

Mon 4   Had another day off. Penny had 1/2 day. So we went out to Inverurie again in afternoon. Had a wonderful time. Brought back loads of flowers & strawberries & raspberries.

Tues 5   Heard from Aberdeen Shipping Co ~ they have a double berth for 23rd Sept. What luck! Met Mardi for tea at Fullers.

Wed 6   Had quite a few letters, cards & telegram from Unc. Penny & I went to see the 'The Brothers' in the evening. Good film but rather depressing.

Sat. 9   Penny & I went rowing on the Dee in morning. Rather a strong current but otherwise quite pleasant. Eat (sic) an enormous meal at West End Cafe afterwards.

Sun 10   Had day off ~ didn't get up until 1.30pm! Then went for cycle ride along Deeside. Had tea out, picked some wild raspberries.

Mon 11   Had evening off. Wrote 6 long letters! Great effort. Have now heard from all Youth Hostels ~ quite ok.

Tues 12   Did some shopping in morning. Letter from Reg, will probably be home end of Sept.

Wed 13   Went to pictures. Saw 'The Courtneys of Curzon St'. Excellent.

West End Cafe ~ in an area of Aberdeen, alongside the River Dee.
Insurance office ~ Holburn Street runs for over 1.5 miles from Aberdeen City Centre to the Bridge of Dee.
Winston Churchill ~ 1874-1965, statesman, soldier, orator, writer and Prime Minister who led Britain during World War II.
Food Kitchens ~ Aberdeen Soup Kitchen, Loch Street, Aberdeen AB25 1DH.

Thurs. 14 *Had first swim in sea this year. Lovely day, but sea was damn cold. Hope this weather holds for our holiday.*

Fri 15 *Went skating in evening with Penny. Met a chap who works in Insurance office in Holburn St. Lugged me around a few times. Bought some chips on the way back.*

Sat. 16 *Started in food Kitchens. Not too bad. Quite enjoyed it. Another lovely day. Heard Winston Churchill speak tonight. Very good speech, in 'good form! But will it do any good?'.*

Tues 26 *Had House written exam. Didn't like paper very much.*

Thurs. 28 *Had Oral & Clinical House exam. Found both much easier than I expected. 61%. Penny got 64%.*

Tues 2 *Had State written exam in morning. Not a bad paper. Had afternoon off ~ Penny & I went shopping.*

---

15 AUGUST: INDIA GAINED INDEPENDENCE WITHIN
THE BRITISH COMMONWEALTH AND SEPARATED INTO
THE SEPARATE DOMINIONS OF PAKISTAN AND INDIA,
BENGAL AND PUNJAB DIVIDED BETWEEN INDIA AND PAKISTAN

24 AUGUST: THE EDINBURGH FESTIVAL OF MUSIC
AND DRAMA LAUNCHED

Wed 3   Got a train to Ballater & stayed night at Youth Hostel. Arrived too late for Warden ~ didn't see him at all.

Thurs 4   Got up early & cycled to Braemar. Loads of traffic all the way. Lester (sic) passed us in coach. Wonderful day ~ saw King & Queen. Enjoyed pipe bands immensely.

Fri 5   Went to pictures in evening. Saw 'Stallion Road'.

Sat. 6   Packed in evening. Also did washing & ironing. As usual got to bed about 12.30am.

Sun 7   Left Foresterhill at 2pm, plus mountains of luggage! Arrived Y.W.C.A. Dee St. in time for tea. Rather peculiar place but we shan't be in very much.

Mon 8   Went shopping in the morning ~ bought rations etc. Took a walk down to the sea & then went to pictures. Did some work before bed.

King & Queen ~ King George VI and Queen Elizabeth (Queen Mother).
Y.W.C.A. Dee St. ~ Young Women's Christian Association, Dee Street, Aberdeen (founded 1902).

Tues **9** Met Morton & Mary at bus stop Dee St at 8.30am for Dundee & arrived 12.30pm. Had nice lunch & went up to Hosp. Awful time waiting for exam but not too bad on the whole. We all passed.

Wed **10** Messed about in morning & finally started for Alford 1.30pm. Had lunch at Loch Skene & then it rained. Arrived Alford about 6pm & stayed at Hotel. Met very nice salesman there. All very friendly over tea at 10.30pm!

Thurs. **11** Awful gale blowing but started for Tomintoul. Very stiff cycling with head wind & hills. Arrived Tomintoul 8.30pm. Wonderful sunset over mountains, lovely run down to Tomintoul.

Fri **12** Wonderful morning. Got some milk in Tomintoul & had good breakfast. Started about 10am for Inverness! Some climb! But managed it ~ wonderful scenery. Arrived 8.30pm.

Sat. 13 *Did some shopping in Inverness & got off about 11am. Rotten head wind again. Arrived Alltsigh about 6pm. Spent an hour lighting stove! Lovely place on shores of Loch Ness.*

Sun 14 *Started for Glen Nevis early ~ quite a long run ~ about 42 miles ~ rained from Fort Augustus onwards. Very big hostel ~ too many people. Ben Nevis surrounded by mists.*

Mon 15 *Got own rations in Fort William and had easy run to Glencoe, over Ballachulish Ferry. Y.H very nice. Had dinner and good wash. Wrote some letters, still raining quite a bit.*

Tues 16 *Started for Crianlarich ~ rain as usual. Got a lift from naval chappie as we were coming thro' Pass of Glencoe. Took us all the way to Crianlarich. Weather cleared up in evening. We went for a walk. Wiebke also there.*

Wed 17 *Quite a good run to Inverbeg. Met Wiebke from time to time. Arrived quite early. I got a lift into Ross and also*

Alltsigh ~ Youth Hostel (1940s-1950s) near Invermoriston, orginally the Half Way House Tea Room.
Stirling Castle ~ Castle Esplanade, Stirling FK8 1EJ.
Bishops Court Hotel ~ possibly the Royal Hotel adjacent to the station.

82

SEPTEMBER 19

19

From 1947 See off for Sandiman Cro
ferry again. Bled pulled tubes home
to Buchanan, on serious meeting an
bottom of Steep hill. Both radiat
bouchy, the fan, had overwork and in
a brewes about help of heavy people in
most of our...

*one coming back! Had a bathe in loch ~ not as cold as
I expected but quite cold enough.*

Thurs 18 *Stayed at Inverbeg and climbed Ben Lomond
with Wiebke, lovely day but we took wrong track up and lost
our way. Rather a stiff climb but worse coming down.
Had to take ferry across Loch Lomond.*

Fri 19 *Set off for Dunblane. Crossed ferry again but piled
bikes up at Balmaha, against railing on bottom of steep hill.
Both rather badly shaken, but otherwise only cuts and bruises.
With help of many people we got to Dunblane about 6pm.
Put bikes on train.*

Sat. 20 *Wandered round Stirling and saw Princess
Elizabeth drive to Stirling Castle. Then caught train to Aberdeen
and put up at Bishops Court Hotel. Wonderful ~ nice meal and
soft bed. Some bad news about boat, will find out more tomorrow.*

Sun 21   *Didn't find out anything as anticipated. Went out to Inverurie. B. was there ~ What a bore! But had good talk with Mrs Johnston.*

Mon 22   *Bank Holiday in Tradeswk* (sic) so shipping office closed! Went up to Foresterhill and said 'Goodbyes'. Went to flicks in evening and met Isabelle.*

Tues 23   *Caught 9am train to Edinburgh. Had an awful time with luggage and money! Wandered round Edinburgh all day and caught night train to London.*

Wed 24   *Arrived here 7am. Had to wake Les up and also to pay Taxi. Spent day unpacking and settling in.*

Thurs 25   *Did loads of washing. Decided to postpone starting at Middlesex till Jan. What rotten luck. I suppose it won't be so bad.*

Sat. 27   *Went over to see Jean and Bill. Did some washing.*

---

22 SEPTEMBER: THE MARSHALL PLAN FOR POST-WAR RECOVERY
   IN EUROPE INAUGURATED BY GEORGE MARSHALL, US SECRETARY
   OF STATE

24 SEPTEMBER: BURMA PROCLAIMED AN INDEPENDENT REPUBLIC

* Unknown. Possible - every third Tuesday in September Princes Day in the Netherlands or Sunday 21 September Swiss Federal Fast (all except GE).

Sun 28 *Les and I went down to Maidenhead by car to tea. Nana has had a stroke. Uncle Ern a bit depressed.*

Mon 29 *Met Bucky for coffee in Knightsbridge. Still same old Bucky! Scandle and Trouble!!*

Wed 1 *Unc came down in evening. Aunt Lil very upset over Pooh, apparently. Reg rang up! Meeting him Mon.*

Thurs 2 *Rang up Somerset in evening. Going down Wed 12.30.*

Sat 4 *Went to June's wedding at Brompton and afterwards Rembrandt Hotel. Very good reception. Got a bit tipsy! Met Mary for tea afterwards.*

Sun 5 *Jean and Bill came to dinner. Managed to cook dinner successfully. All went down in car to Maidenhead for tea.*

Mon 6 *Reg in bed with tonsillitus. Too bad! Peg came up in evening.*

Brompton ~ Brompton Oratory, Brompton Road,
City of London, Greater London SW7 2RP.
Rembrandt Hotel ~ 11, Thurloe Place, London SW7 2RS.

Tues 7 *Peg and I went out in morning and had coffee. Les and Peg went up to town. I did some ironing and later some packing.*

Wed 8 *Somerset.*

Fri 5 *Met Nance & Aunt Lil at Marble Arch. We booked some seats, had tea & then came home.*

Sat. 6 *Nance and I went up Putney in afternoon. Bought some Penguin crime books to read.!*

Sun 7 *Quiet day. Peg came up in evening.*

Mon 8 *Nance and I went to Hippodrome in afternoon to see 'Technicolour Wedding' film, also 'Woman in the Halls'.*

Tues 9 *Went over to Jean's for tea.*

Wed 10 *Went to see 'Off the Record' at Piccadilly. Very good. Had tea out beforehand and did some shopping.*

13 OCTOBER: DEATH OF THE SOCIALIST AND AUTHOR SIDNEY WEBB

17 OCTOBER: BURMA LEFT THE BRITISH COMMONWEALTH

20 NOVEMBER: MARRIAGE OF PRINCESS ELIZABETH AND PHILIP, LIEUTENANT PHILIP MOUNTBATTEN, R.N. (PRINCE PHILIP OF GREECE). GIVEN THE TITLE OF H.R.H THE DUKE OF EDINBURGH

Thurs 11 Went to the Ice Hockey match at Wembley. Between
England and Czechoslovakia. Good Match. England lost 9-3.

Fri 12 Went to Peter Jones to do some Xmas shopping
and had tea there.

Sat. 13 Nance and I went to see 'Barber of Serville'
at Cambridge Theatre. Enjoyed it very much.

Sun 14 Jean and Bill came to dinner and Peg turned
up for tea. Had to move all furniture out of front bedroom
~ decorators coming in ~ what fun!

Mon 15 Saw Nance off at Paddington. Seems to have
enjoyed her week. Not looking forward to going back!

Tues 16 Went skating with Joyce and Margery.

Wed 17 Did remainder of my Xmas shopping. Quite lucky.
Rang Unc up in evening. Met Mary by chance in Oxford St.

---

11 DECEMBER: ICE HOCKEY MATCH, WEMBLEY
14 DECEMBER: DEATH OF STANLEY BALDWIN, EARL BALDWIN
OF BEWDLEY

Wembley ~ Wembley Stadium, a major sports and entertainment venue.
Peter Jones ~ Department store, Sloane Square, London SW1W 8EL.
Paddington ~ Paddington Station, the London terminus of the Great Western Railway.

Thurs 18   Went out to tea with Unc, and did some shopping. Then went to see 'Ideal Husband' and had supper at Granby Inn.

Fri 19   Had busy day. Did some shopping up Putney for Les. Trying hard to finish Peg's Xmas present.

Sat. 20   Had another busy day. Scrubbed front bedroom and then polished floor. Did Xmas parcels and cards.

Sun 21   Went up to cemetery with Les and then back and moved furniture back in front bedroom. Peg arrived in evening.

Mon 22   Peg went off in evening. Washed my hair.

Tues 23   Busy day. Workmen went in evening.

Wed 24   Had very busy day ~ polishing and cooking etc. Put decorations up in evening with help of Mr. Johnstone. Also candles on mantlepiece.

Thurs. 25   Didn't get up very early, I got early morning tea!

Granby Inn ~ a dining public house, possibly in the Fulham or Putney area.

Les & Bill went to football while Jean and I endeavoured to get turkey in oven! Dinner cooked very nicely ~ had presents just before. Played Monopoly in evening.

26 *Had a lay in ~ then Jean and I cooked dinner etc. Peg arrived for dinner. Lit candles in evening ~ very pretty!*

27 *Developed toothache ~ thought this would come after the earache. Tried to get rid of it by Veganin. Felt pretty miserable. Went to pictures with Jean and Bill in afternoon.*

28 *Still had toothache! Had chicken for dinner. Peg stayed night but Jean and Bill went home.*

29 *Went to Dentist but have got to have gas? abscess. Not till Wed, though.*

30 *Usual.*

31 *Had tooth out with gas! Didn't feel too (sic) in evening and nearly passed out at 11.45pm! Had to have Brandy.*

Monopoly ~ a popular board game, once used by British Secret Service in WWII.
Veganin ~ prescribed for headaches, as recommended by The British Journal of Nursing, December 1947.

*Mid winter views of
The Close, surrounding
land and fields.*

Gentleman Farmer! Unc.

*The Close at Wedmore,
Aunt Lil and Pooh,
Barb, sheep!*

View from my bedroom of Foresterhill

View from my window, March 1947   *Foresterhill*

On the hill behind hospital

*"Went out in snow
in the morning.
Took some photographs."*

From right: Duncan, Barb, Naryn (sic), Hope, Stables, Patience

Penny, Aberdeen beach

S/N Milne with 'George' & self

MAR LODGE, BRAEMAR

*"Walked right into grounds
& into Castle as the painters had
gone to lunch & left the door open!
Then went to Braemars."*

PENNY, TAKEN BY RIVER DEE
AT BALMORAL

CRATHIE CHURCH (BALMORAL)

LODGE AND LODGE GATES

"Cycled to Loch Skene in afternoon. Had a wonderful ride. Took some photos."

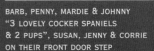

BARB, PENNY, MARDIE & JOHNNY
"3 LOVELY COCKER SPANIELS
& 2 PUPS", SUSAN, JENNY & CORRIE
ON THEIR FRONT DOOR STEP

The front of
The Old Vicarage
viewed from the
street wall

View of St Mary's Church
across the road from
The Old Vicarage

Views of the
back garden at
The Old Vicarage

Nance sitting under
the thatch canopy
in the shade

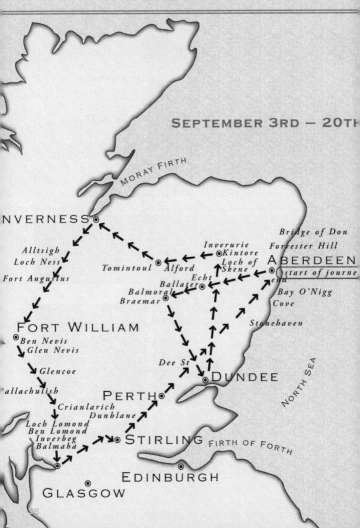

SEPTEMBER 3RD – 20TH

MORAY FIRTH

INVERNESS

Alltsigh
Loch Ness
Fort Augustus

Tomintoul *Alford*

Inverurie
Kintore
Loch of
Skene

Bridge of Don
Forrester Hill

ABERDEEN
start of journey

Echt
Ballater
Balmoral
Braemar

end

Bay O'Nigg
Cove

Stonehaven

FORT WILLIAM

Ben Nevis
Glen Nevis

Glencoe

Ballachulish

Crianlarich
Dunblane

Loch Lomond
Ben Lomond
Inverbeg
Balmaha

Dee St

DUNDEE

NORTH SEA

PERTH

STIRLING FIRTH OF FORTH

EDINBURGH

GLASGOW

BRAEMAR GATHERING, SEPT. 1947

LOCH SKENE WITH LODGE GATES IN BACKGROUND, BARB

PENNY ON LOCH SKENE

GLENN, NEAR TOMINTOUL

99

Invermoriston, bottom of Loch Ness

GLENCOE (IN ITS USUAL GARB)

ISABELLE

LOCH NESS

*"Started for Crianlarich ~
rain as usual. Got a lift from
naval chappie as we were
coming thro' Pass of Glencoe.
Took us all the way to Crianlarich."*

*"Wandered round Edinburgh
all day and caught night
train to London."*

SCOTT MEMORIAL IN PRINCES ST. EDINBURGH

VIEW FROM CASTLE, PRINCES STREET

EDINBURGH CASTLE

FRONT OF CASTLE & SENTRY

BARB, EDINBURGH CASTLE

PENNY, MON'S MEG

HISTORICAL AND SOCIAL EVENTS DURING 1948
Extracts taken from ~ *Chronology of British History,* Brockhampton Reference/Press.

104

JANUARY 1948

HISTORICAL AND SOCIAL EVENTS DURING 1948

- THE INDEPENDENT LABOUR PARTY CEASED TO HAVE
  PARLIAMENTARY REPRESENTATION
- BRITISH UNION OF FASCISTS REVIVED BY SIR OSWALD MOSLEY
- PLURAL VOTING DISCONTINUED BY ACT OF PARLIAMENT

Thurs. 1 *Toothache better but still there. Wrote some letters & did some needlework!*

Sun 15 *Arrived back Middlesex Hosp in evening. Saw Brenda. Mary away for nights off. No idea where I am going.*

Mon 16 *Started work as Staff nurse. Went to Matron at 8.30 ~ To go on night duty. What fun! Acting Night Sister ~ on Meyerstein Wing.*

Tues 17 *Mackie is on night duty ~ had a shock when she saw me. Also Bertwhistle & Sloggett.*

Mon 1 *Mary went before the Committee re getting her blues. Pretty certain but decision withheld.*

Sat. 6 *Mary getting her blues on April 1st.*

Fri 19 *On Woolavington Wing. What a joke! Last time I was here was on 2nd floor with Mardi.*

---

1 **JANUARY:** RAILWAYS AMALGAMATE UNDER NATIONAL OWNERSHIP

4 **JANUARY:** BURMA GAINS INDEPENDENCE, LEAVING COMMONWEALTH

12 **JANUARY:** OPENING OF THE FIRST
SUPERMARKET IN BRITAIN, (LONDON)

4 **FEBRUARY:** CEYLON BECAME A DOMINION
WITHIN THE BRITISH COMMONWEALTH

Mon 22 *Still on Woolavington Wing. Bored. Saw Weston in the morning ~ she is doing private nursing and making quite a packet! Val Hudson having a baby!*

Tues 23 *Didn't go out. Wrote some letters.*

Fri 26 *Had 6 nights off. Arrived home & went to sleep ...!!*

Sat. 27 *Boat Race ~ Cambridge wins again. Joyce and I watched. Had tea at Peg's and then went to pictures.*

Sun 28 *Jean & Bill came over to Putney.*

Mon 29 *Spent day with Peg & Les. Messed about. Went back to Manor Park in evening.*

Thurs 1 *Back on duty after 6 nights off. Now on Woola ~ S/Parker's holiday.*

Mon 12 *Last night on Woolavington Wing. S/Parker back tonight. May have to go down to York House.*

27 MARCH: BOAT RACE, CAMBRIDGE WINS AGAIN

1 APRIL: ELECTRICITY INDUSTRY NATIONALIZED

Boat Race, Blakes Wharves

Commitee. blues ~ when a nurse qualifies.
Manor Park ~ Nurses home or Jean & Bill's home.
York House ~ relating to The Middlesex Hospital.

Tues 13 *Nights off! Spent the day with Joyce at Barnes. Lovely day. Haven't got to go down to York. The 4 of us may remain here.*

Wed 14 *Messed about. Went to see new Roosevelt Statue in Grosvenor Square. Looks very fine.*

Thurs 15 *Went out to coffee with Mardi and Thornton. Met Joyce in afternoon for some shopping ~ didn't do any! Went to see 'Spring in Park Lane'. Very good.*

Fri 16 *Went out to coffee with Penny ~ she has been offered her blues ~ N/Sister Woolavington Wing! What a hoot ~ she has refused of course. Went down to Putney and took some flowers to the grave.*

Sat. 24 *Joyce came up & we went swimming. Had coffee afterwards & discussed Denmark. Have not heard anything yet.*

16 APRIL: ESTABLISHMENT OF THE ORGANISATION FOR EUROPEAN ECONOMIC COOPERATION (OEEC)

• INSTITUTE OF CONTEMPORARY ARTS FOUNDED

Roosevelt Statue ~ unveiled on 12th April, it had been funded entirely through the sale of a souvenir brochure to the British public.

APRIL 1948

Sun 25 *Nights off. Went out to Penny's. Felt rather tired & sleepy. Ronald & Val came round & Penny. Spent most of her time with children. Came back in evening.*

Mon 26 *Mardi & I went to Carlton House in morning to see Royal Procession. Excellent view, took some snaps. Saw 'Chiltern Hundreds' in the evening. Very good.*

Tues 27 *Did some ironing etc. Went to see 'Snowbound' in evening. Very good picture.*

Wed 28 *Messed about all day & waited for Penny to come off in evening. Eventually arrived at 5.45pm! Went to News Reel & saw 'Silver Wedding'. Penny very miserable these days.*

Thurs 29 *Went out to coffee with Thornton in morning. Had letter from Joyce. H.Y, particulars have come through at last. For the 25th August.*

- KING GEORGE VI AND QUEEN ELIZABETH
  CELEBRATE SILVER WEDDING ANNIVERSARY

Carlton House ~ near St. James between Pall Mall and The Mall.
Royal Procession ~ a brigade of guards lined the Mall to Admiralty Arch with cheering crowds, waving flags and handkerchiefs. Their Majesties saluted and waved almost continuously, the flags of a nation flew over buildings, hiding many war scars.

Tues 11   *S/N Paine on night duty with us. Also Sister Haines.*

Sat. 29   *On Woola.*

Sun 30   *On Woola.*

Mon 31   *Had a night in the 'office'. Hockey came on to do Woola, so I was out of a job for one night.*

Tues 1   *Paine off tonight ~ I am on Meyerstein Wing. Went to 'Trade Show' at Warner awful film ~ thoroughly bored.*

Wed 2   *Went out with Hockey to arrange for a wireless from Radio Rentals. Will send it tomorrow.*

Thurs. 3   *Went out to coffee with Thornton. Came back fairly early. At last I've found out who is to be our new night superintendent ~ Sister Brown. S/Johnson will be disappointed! I'm really very sorry for her.*

---

14 MAY: PALESTINE PARTIONED, THE NEW STATE OF ISRAEL FORMED
18 JUNE: RUSSIAN BLOCKADE OF BERLIN: WESTERN SUPPLIES AIRLIFT
22 JUNE: POST WAR IMMIGRATION FROM THE COMMONWEALTH BEGINS
5 JULY: THE NATIONAL HEALTH SERVICE CAME INTO EFFECT

Radio Rentals ~ its radios were made usually by E.K. Cole Ltd (who made 'Ekco' radios) or Mains Radios and Gramophones Ltd, a Yorkshire firm, which it acquired in 1945.

Fri 4   *Still waiting to have wireless fixed up. Have no flex. Hope our electricians have some.*

Thurs 29   *Went to opening Ceremony of Olympics with Caine & Johnson. Had a wonderful time. Didn't have any sleep but was well worth it.*

Sat. 31   *Nights off ~ Went home to Manor Park. Went to sleep!*

Sun 1   *Went down to Chatham with Joyce & met Sam & Cecil for the day. Very hot. Went back to ship for dinner, had some drinks & then went back to Putney.*

Mon 2   *Over at Putney. Intended going to Olympic swimming but poured with rain & didn't go.*

Tues 3   *Did some shopping & bought a 'Winproof' with Les' coupons. Quiet evening!*

---

15 JULY: ALCOHOLICS ANONYMOUS FOUNDED IN BRITAIN

29 JULY: BREAD RATIONING ENDED

29 JULY: OPENING OF THE FOURTEENTH OFFICIAL MODERN OLYMPIC GAMES IN LONDON. FANNY BLANKERS-KOEN WINS FOUR GOLD MEDALS

Winproof ~ lightweight raincoat bought with clothing rationing coupons, clothes rationing ending in March 1949.

Wed 4   *Back on duty. Went down to Putney in afternoon for tea.*

Fri 6   *Had a late pass & went out with Mary in evening. Then had a party in the office at 10.30 & a few drinks!. I was on Woola.*

Tues 10   *Had a swim in the morning.*

Mon 16   *Went to International Horse Show with Flossie. Very interesting.*

Tues 17   *Did odd jobs in morning. Had tea out with Mary in afternoon. Washed hair & dyed skirt in evening.*

Wed 18   *Back from night off. Was extra, just messed about.*

Thurs 19   *Played tennis in morning. On 4th floor Woola at night. Went to Bank & collected my Travellers cheques & Danish money.*

Joyce & Babs

16 AUGUST: INTERNATIONAL HORSE SHOW
- COLD WAR BEGAN
- IRAQ, ISRAEL AND KOREA GIVE VOTES TO WOMEN

International Horse Show ~ at White City Stadium, London.

Fri 20 *Spent the night on 4th floor Woola. Had quite a good time ~ no losses & 1 1/2 hrs rest! Did washing in morning & asked Anglefor (sic) about bike in room ~ she was rather staggered but said yes.*

Mon 23 *Last night! Still on Woola. Not much to do.*

Tues 24 *Night off. Went out with Joyce in afternoon after sleeping in morning. Went to pictures with K. Caine in evening & saw 'London Belongs to Me'. Very good. Then did some packing & fused the lights!*

Wed 25 *Cycled to Liverpool St. Only another girl Ann Warmsley & ourselves going. Will be rather fun on our own. Went on board at 1pm. Rather an old tub of a boat! Sea quite rough. Met Stewart Chamberlayne & Angus Mackay!*

Liverpool St. ~ is the London terminus of the former Great Eastern Railway, originally providing routes to Norwich via Ipswich, Kings Lynn via Cambridge.

Thurs 26 *Very rough night & had funny time at breakfast as ship was rolling quite a bit. Got in to Esbjerg 1pm & had lunch there with the boys & then cycled to Ribe, only ones in Hostel. Had large supper at Hotel.*

Fri 27 *Decided to part company with the boys ~ to avoid complications! We cycled to Kolding. Met some American girls. Walked through Kolding & had coffee & cakes at wonderful restaurant ~ Salteshess (sic).*

Sat. 28 *Went over Koldinghus Castle in morning, partially burnt down. Also saw Gestapo cell. Then cycled to Assens crossed Little Belt Bridge. Very beautiful. Had meal out.*

Sun 29 *Cycled to Korsor via Odense & Gt. Belt ferry. Saw statue of house & gardens of H. Andersen. Enjoyed the ferry from Nyberg to Korsor & arrived at very nice hostel. Looked at harbour lights after dark!*

- DAME LILIAN PENSON, FIRST WOMAN VICE-CHANCELLOR OF THE UNIVERSITY OF LONDON
- CAMBRIDGE UNIVERSITY OPENS ITS FULL DEGREES TO WOMEN

Gestapo cell ~ the only remaining cell from Gestapo activities in Denmark
H. Andersen ~ Hans Christian Andersen, a Danish author, fairy tale writer and poet noted for his children's stories.

Mon 30 *Had a look round Korsor & I bought a little cover for Jean. Then cycled to Roskilde & had quite a job finding the place. Fell downstairs & sprained my ankle! Strapped it up with cold compresses etc.*

Tues 31 *D.W.H. 'Horsgaarden' (sic) very beautiful outside but appalling privy (sic) midden in the yard! Cycled to Kobenhavn, ankle not too bad. Went to Tivoli & Christiansborg Palace & harbour. Very tired.*

Wed 1 *Went to Sweden, Malmo for the day. Saw Mr Fehling of the Private Bank, Borsgade & he managed some Swedish crowns! Everything very expensive in Malmo but I bought some films. Met Danish man who took our photographs and then came back on the boat with him and about 6-12 schoolboys! We smuggled some tea through the customs for him.*

- JOYCE BOUGHT A LIBERTY BODICE FOR HER SISTER, JUNE'S FIRST BORN
- COVER ~ BOUGHT FOR JEAN'S BABY BOY

Midden ~ a dung heap, dunghill.
Private Bank ~ Privatbanken, founded in 1857 under the directorship of C.F. Tietgen. A monumental, Baroque-style building behind the Børsgade. Privatbanken was the first bank in Denmark to introduce the use of cheques.

Thurs 2 *Learned that the boys had arrived in Copenhagen ~ had been to the night spots! Took bikes down to harbour & got our tickets. Then did some shopping & saw Amalienborg Castle & Mermaid. Went to Elsinore in evening & then caught night boat to Aarhus.*

Fri 3 *Had a wonderful night, a real bed on bunk. Slept very well ~ ship didn't roll, landed at 7.30am & had breakfast. Then went to Den Gamle By, The Old Town & the New University & Marselisborg Castle & then to Silkeborg.*

Sat. 4 *Poured with rain, I got a puncture which I stuck up with glue! Arrived Horsens wet through & miserable. Had a wonderful supper & went to bed early.*

Sun 5 *Weather cleared up, cycled to Vejle, very easy day. Went round the harbour & fjord. Boys turned up in evening & then went off again? with 2 Belgian girls !! Awful night ~ noisy.*

- ELEANOR ROOSEVELT PLAYS A KEY ROLE IN THE DRAFTING OF THE UNIVERSAL DECLARATION OF HUMAN RIGHTS
- THE MALAYAN UNION BECAME THE FEDERATION OF MALAYA

Mon 6   Started off for Bramminge & then it started to rain ~ simply poured. Thoroughly soaked, so got a bus to Kilm (sic) out of Bramminge. Wonderful Y.H. Had to pump own water from well! House is haunted! Stew & Gus turned up 10.30pm.

Tues 7   Didn't get up until 8.45am. Had bacon & eggs for breakfast. Cycled to Esbjerg ~ where I fell off my bike & grazed my knee quite badly! Had wonderful lunch & did some shopping. Caught boat at 6pm. Rough night.

Wed 8   Sea still rough ~ boat pitching & tossing instead of rolling, felt rather 'uneasy'! Arrived Harwich 8.15pm. Cycled back to Hosp & arrived 12.15am, had dinner with S/Brown, & Jordan. Had a bath! To bed at 2.15am!

Thurs 9   Got up late, had a long chat with Ruth. On duty! And on Maternity. Fed up with life. Stew didn't ring until 11pm ~ couldn't get through.

- ART DIRECTOR CARMEN DILLON WINS AN OSCAR FOR HER SET DESIGNS FOR LAURENCE OLIVIER'S FILM, HAMLET

Y.H. ~ a (haunted) Youth Hostel.

Fri 10   *Furious at being put on Maternity but can't do much about it.*

Sun 12   *Got up in afternoon & went down to Stew's place in Putney. Nice family.*

Mon 13   *Had nights off ~ 2. Went home & slept!*

Tues 14   *Met Stew in afternoon & went out to Chipstead & had tea there. Lovely day, went to pictures in evening & saw 'I Remember Mama' Very good.*

Wed 15   *Developed a heavy cold. Slept most of day. On duty at night on West Wing.*

Sat. 18   *Got up & had tea with Stew at S & F. Very short afternoon.*

Mon 20   *Went to R.M.O about my ankle & had it x.rayed.*

---

28 SEPTEMBER: FIRST BRITISH GRAND PRIX RUN AT SILVERSTONE

S & F ~ Special Forces Club.
R.M.O ~ Resident Medical Officer.

Mon 4   *Went up to Rosalind Chetwynd.*

Fri 8   *Not liking day duty very much but I guess I will later on.*

Mon 18   *Stew & I are not getting on very well ~ don't really seem to suit ~ except physically.*

Tues 2   *Stew & I have been talking about marriage ~ I am by no means certain.*

Wed 3   *I'm afraid we are rushing things too much ~ as least he is ~ I know it's not wise ~ but he doesn't seem to have much sense about these things.*

Sun 21   *Stew & I have decided to give it up. I'm very relieved. Kevin Read is getting rather interested.*

Mon 22   *Have been out with Kevin Read. I feel I can hardly trust myself. First one & then the other!*

---

12 OCTOBER: PRODUCTION BEGAN OF THE MORRIS MINOR CAR
   DESIGNED BY ALEX ISSIGONIS
14 NOVEMBER: BIRTH OF CHARLES, PRINCE OF WALES
   DECEMBER: JAM RATIONING ENDED
31 DECEMBER: DEATH OF SIR MALCOLM CAMPBELL

LES AND PEG AT THEIR
WEDDING ON SUNDAY
8TH FEBRUARY, 1948.
BARB, MAIDENHEAD,
BERKSHIRE

*"Mardi & I went to
Carlton House in
morning to see Royal
Procession. Excellent
view, took some snaps."*

ROYAL PROCESSION,
SILVER WEDDING ANNIVERSARY
OF THE KING & QUEEN

ROOSEVELT
STATUE,
GROSVENOR
SQUARE,
LONDON

DENMARK

"Walked through Kolding & had coffee & cakes..."

ANN, BARB & JOYCE
THE GIRLS POOLED THEIR
MONEY. ASKED IF THEY HAD
ENOUGH FOR A CUP OF COFFEE
AND A CAKE. AT FIRST — SAID
ONLY COFFEE AND THEN
ALRIGHT PERHAPS COULD
MANAGE A CAKE AS WELL.

AUGUST 25TH – SEPTEMBER 8TH

*The journey – a train
from Liverpool Street
Station to Harwich,
then a boat (steerage)
through the Straits
of Dover, across
the North Sea
to Esbjerg,
Denmark.*

SKAGERRAK

NORTH SEA

KATTEGAT

DENMARK

SWEDEN

Silkeborg

Aarhus

Helsingör

Horsens

Bramminge *Vejle*

end

Esbjerg
Kolding
Ribe

Odense

Tivoli

KØBENHAVN

Roskilde

Malmo

start of journey

Lille Bælt
Assens
Nyborg

Korsför

BALTIC SEA

Denmark 1948

ON BOARD SHIP EN ROUTE
FOR DENMARK — WENT STEERAGE

ESBJERG

*"Rather an old tub of a boat!
Sea quite rough... Got into
Esbjerg 1pm & had lunch there
with the boys & then cycled
to Ribe."*

GROUP: UNKNOWN GIRL, ANN,
STEWART, BABS & ANGUS;

GROUP: ANGUS, JOYCE
AND STEWART; BOYS — ONE WAS
A TRAINEE CHEF AT THE RITZ,
ONE WAS A MEDICAL STUDENT

122

RIBE, FROM CHURCH TOWER

BABS & ANN, KOLINGE,
TOP OF TOWER

*"Went over Koldinghus
Castle in morning,
partially burnt down.
Also saw Gestapo cell."*

JOYCE & ANN ON BRIDGE   BABS & ANN, ODENSE   ROSKILDE CASTLE

*The Harbour,
Copenhagen*

"Saw Mr Fehling of the Private Bank, Borsgade & he managed some Swedish crowns!"

THE TRANSFER OF MONEY WAS NOT ALLOWED. A BANK MANAGER ON BOARD THE BOAT GAVE THEM ABOUT ONE POUNDS WORTH OF SWEDISH CROWNS, AS THEY HAD NO SWEDISH MONEY.

BABS, MALMÖ

SWEDISH COASTLINE FROM ELSINORE

YACHT PASSED ON OUR RETURN FROM SWEDEN

ELSINORE CASTLE.
TOP RIGHT: ANN AND JOYCE

SENTRY OUTSIDE KING'S CASTLE IN COPENHAGEN, DENMARK 1948

JOYCE

BRAMMINGE YOUTH HOSTEL

"Started off for Bramminge
& then it started to rain ...
wonderful Y.H. Had to pump
own water from well!
House is haunted!"

LEAVING ESBJERG

VEJLE, DANISH CHURCH

SISTER J. BALL

STAFF AND MR ROQUES, ROSALIND CHETWYND, XMAS 1948

FRANK DENNY, 'BARMAN'!

SISTER GRANT
AND DAVID DONALDSON

MR JACKSON AND HIS SON
IN MATERNITY

S/N BARBARA RUSSELL
– CHRISTMAS 1948

MR. ROQUES CARVING THE
TURKEY

HISTORICAL AND SOCIAL EVENTS DURING 1949
Extracts taken from ~ *Chronology of British History*, Brockhampton Reference/Press.

130

JANUARY 1949

HISTORICAL AND SOCIAL EVENTS DURING 1949

9 JANUARY: DEATH OF THE COMEDIAN TOMMY HANDLEY

- THE ATS (AUXILIARY TERRITORIAL SERVICE) WAS TRANSFORMED INTO A PERMANENT FORCE, THE WOMEN'S ROYAL ARMY CORPS, (WRAC)
- FIRST APPEARANCE OF THE GOON SHOW COMEDY SERIES ON BBC RADIO

Tues 15 *Went to office about special leave for next week when Peg goes away. Allowed special leave. Holiday postponed.*

Wed 16 *Had a long aft. Did some general cleaning up. When John & I were in Stewards office Matron & Dickie Bird came in. Didn't say a word!*

Mon 28 *Spent day with Peg & Les. Messed about. Went back to Manor Park in evening.*

Thurs. 31 *Back on duty after 6 nights off. Now on Woola ~ S/Parker's holiday.*

Thurs 28 *Nance died 3am today.*

Fri 29 *Sent off some flowers. Funeral on Monday in Somerset.*

Nance and Barb

15 MARCH: END OF CLOTHES RATIONING

4 APRIL: NORTH ATLANTIC TREATY (NATO) ORGANISATION SIGNED IN WASHINGTON DC. MUTUAL DEFENCE PACT BETWEEN EUROPEAN NATIONS AND THE USA

18 APRIL: EIRE LEAVES BRITISH COMMONWEALTH, REPUBLIC OF IRELAND COMES INTO BEING

MAIDENHEAD, SUMMER 1949

Barb & John,
Manor Park, Barb on gate,
Thames ~ Barb & Jean,
Maidenhead ~ Peg
& Uncle Ern

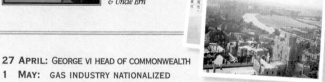

Windsor Castle & grounds

27 APRIL: GEORGE VI HEAD OF COMMONWEALTH

1 MAY: GAS INDUSTRY NATIONALIZED

5 MAY: COUNCIL OF EUROPE CAME INTO EFFECT

13 MAY: TEST FLIGHT OF THE CANBERRA JET BOMBER

8 JUNE: PUBLICATION OF 1984 BY GEORGE ORWELL

29 JULY: WEATHER FORECAST FIRST TELEVISED

Marjorie, Joyce & Barb
~ Gyllynvase Beach,
Falmouth, Cornwall

John and I on Rottingdeane beach 1949

St. Ives

Norway Cottage

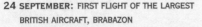

John

24 SEPTEMBER: FIRST FLIGHT OF THE LARGEST BRITISH AIRCRAFT, BRABAZON

6 OCTOBER: BERLIN BLOCKADE LIFTED

- SET UP OF THE NATURE CONSERVANCY
- PLANS ANNOUNCED FOR TWELVE NATIONAL PARKS IN ENGLAND & WALES
- ROSE HEILBRON BECOMES THE FIRST WOMAN KING'S COUNSEL

Tuberculosis may be as old as the Earth itself, first infecting animals ~ possibly inhaled or ingested from the soil. It would have been passed on to humans through the animals' flesh and milk. It affected many kinds of animals including cows, birds, fish and reptiles. From 4000 BC examinations of the spines of mummies and tomb paintings in Egypt and skeletal remains in Italy show the earliest evidence of TB in the human spine. A neolithic grave near Heidleberg, Germany, dating back to 5000 BC also confirms TB as a common disease.

Established in mainland Europe around 2500 BC ~ 1500 BC, the earliest evidence of the disease in Britain comes from graves dating from the Roman occupation (55 BC ~ 800 AD). One in five deaths in London by the mid 17th Century, recorded in the Bills of Mortality were due to TB consumption. Fast becoming an epidemic in Britain and in the USA and Europe TB became known as the 'White Plague'.

*General Register Office Certificates: Births, Deaths & Marriages.

136

- *19th Century, London and New York, two of the worst affected cities.*

- *1882, Germany, Dr Robert Koch discovered the bacterial cause of TB.*

- *1931, France, Drs Calmette and Guerin discovered Bacillus Calmett-Guerin (BCG) a 'tamed' living bacterium.*

- *1942, USA, Drs Feldman and Hinshaw reported the first drug trial (Promin) in the treatment of TB.*

- *1944, January, Drs Schatz, Bugie and Waksman announced the discovery of a drug called 'Streptomycin'. A 21 year old woman was the first patient to be successfully treated.*

- *Post 1945, Streptomycin, found in chickens, was also capable of treating many other diseases that penicillin could not. Too much use, led to the germ developing a resistance.*

- *1946, Dr Lehmann published a paper concerning the discovery of Para-Amino-Salicylic (PAS).*

DEATH CERTIFICATE OF NANCY WINIFRED HOLE
3 JANUARY 1923 — 28 APRIL 1949.
OCCUPATION OF DECEASED — SPINSTER, TRAINEE NURSE. AGE 26 YEARS
AT THE MOUNT VERNON HOSPITAL, RUISLIP, NORTHWOOD.
CAUSE OF DEATH: 1A.RENAL FAILURE (KIDNEY), 1B. AMYLOID DISEASE,
1C. TUBERCULOSIS, ABCESS OF THE SPINE

*The Mantoux Test, devised by Charles Mantoux (1877~1947)
was an injection to test for TB. The Patch test was a method
of testing on children. The Tuberculin, was rubbed into the
skin and the appearance of a weal, within 48 hours under
the skin confirmed the presence of tuberculosis.*

- *1950, Britain adopted a vaccination programme for
children aged 11, together with a BCG vaccine and regular
chest x-rays.*

- *1960, Dr John Crofton a TB expert at the University of
Edinburgh proposed a combination of drugs and declared
'all out war' to conquer the disease. By the 1970's, five
antibiotics existed which could be used to fight against TB.*

- *A decline continued for 40 years but now with world
wide migration, open borders and no cursory health
checks many countries are again blighted by TB. Once
more, the intention is to stop the disease from taking
a hold in this country.*

TUBERCULOSIS – AN INFECTIOUS, COMMUNICABLE DISEASE, CAUSED
BY BACTERIUM. MOST FREQUENTLY INFECTING THE LUNGS BUT MAY ALSO
INVOLVE THE LARYNX, BONES AND JOINTS, SKIN, LYMPH NODES,
INTESTINES, KIDNEYS AND THE NERVOUS SYSTEM.

Extracts from ~ *Illustrated Family Medical Encyclopaedia.* The Readers Digest Association
Limited. *Principles of Medicine and Medical Nursing,* Hodder & Stoughton.
Pulmonary Tuberculosis ~ Originally by Frederick Marais.

THE OLYMPIC GAMES, 1948

LONDON WAS ORIGINALLY GRANTED THE 1944 EVENT BUT COULD NOT ACT AS HOST BECAUSE OF WWII. THE SO CALLED AUSTERITY GAMES, THREE YEARS AFTER THE SECOND WORLD WAR, WERE STAGED ON A BUDGET OF £761,000 ALTHOUGH £5 MILLION MORE WAS SPENT IMPROVING THE CITY'S INFRASTRUCTURE.

WHEN MEDICAL STUDENT JOHN MARK BORE THE OLYMPIC FLAME INTO WEMBLEY IN JULY 1948, IT WAS THE START OF AN EVENT WHICH WOULD BE INCONCEIVABLE TO THE ATHLETES OF TODAY. NONE OF THE 4,099 COMPETITORS WAS A PROFESSIONAL ATHLETE, WITH MOST HAVING TO HOLD DOWN FULL-TIME JOBS TO SUBSIDISE THEIR SPORT. TWO WEEKS BEFORE THE EVENT, BRITISH COMPETITORS WERE GIVEN INCREASED FOOD RATIONS IN THE HOPE OF BOOSTING THEIR PERFORMANCE. THERE WERE NO SPECIALLY BUILT OLYMPIC VILLAGES TO ACCOMMODATE THE ATHLETES, INSTEAD THEY WERE HOUSED IN THE CONVERTED CLASSROOMS OF MIDDLESEX SCHOOLS, AS WELL AS ACCOMMODATION IN RICHMOND PARK, RAF UXBRIDGE AND WEST DRAYTON.

FED PLATES OF EGG AND HAM, THEY HAD TO MAKE DO WITH RUBBER PLIMSOLLS AND MANY EVEN WALKED TO THEIR EVENTS AT THE MAIN VENUE, WEMBLEY STADIUM.

DISTANCE RUNNERS EMIL ZATOPEK AND FANNY BLANKERS-KOEN WERE THE STARS ON A CINDER TRACK OVER A GRASS SURROUND. THE DUTCH HOUSE-WIFE WON FOUR GOLD MEDALS, WHILE ZATOPEK SMASHED THE OLYMPIC RECORD FOR 10,000 METRES.

A HANDFUL OF SPORTS, SUCH AS YACHTING, RIDING, ROWING, BASKET-BALL AND CYCLING, WERE HELD AT OTHER CENTRES, SUCH AS THE OUTDOORS VELODROME AT HERNE HILL USED FOR CYCLING EVENTS. ROWER BERT BUSHNELL WON ONE OF THREE BRITISH GOLD MEDALS IN 1948, BUT RETIRED FROM THE SPORT SOON AFTER TO CONCENTRATE ON HIS JOB AS A MARINE ENGINEER. AS HE SAID:

'IT WAS THE CASE THAT YOU HAD TO GO TO WORK — AND WORK AND ROWING DIDN'T REALLY MIX.'

'Class of '48', article and image from The Daily Mail relating to the Olympic Games held in London in 1948.

In 1935, you needed either a lot of money or a library card if you wanted to read a good book. Cheap paperbacks were available but their poor production generally tended to mirror the quality between the covers.

Penguin paperbacks were the brainchild of Allen Lane, then a director of The Bodley Head. After a weekend visiting Agatha Christie in Devon, he found himself on a platform at Exeter station searching its bookstall for something to read on his journey back to London but discovered only popular magazines and reprints of Victorian novels.

Appalled by the selection on offer, Lane decided that good quality contemporary fiction should be made available at an attractive price and sold not just in traditional bookshops but also in railway stations, tobacconists and chain stores. He also wanted a 'dignified but flippant' symbol for his new business. His secretary suggested a Penguin and another

employee was sent to London Zoo to make some sketches. Seventy years later Penguin is still one of the most recognizable brands in the world. The first Penguin paperbacks appeared in the summer of 1935 and included works by Ernest Hemingway, André Maurois and Agatha Christie.

The paperbacks were colour coded (orange for fiction, blue for biography, green for crime) and cost just sixpence, the same price as a packet of cigarettes. The way the public thought about books changed forever ~ the paperback revolution had begun.

"We believed in the existence in this country of a vast reading public for intelligent books at a low price, and staked everything on it." Allen Lane.

Penguin became a separate company in 1936 and set up premises in the Crypt of the Holy Trinity Church on Marylebone Road, using a fairground slide to receive deliveries from the street above. Within twelve months, it had sold a staggering 3 million paperbacks. Traditional publishers tended to view Penguin with suspicion and uncertainty, as did some authors.

"The Penguin Books are splendid value for sixpence, so splendid that if other publishers had any sense they would combine against them and suppress them." George Orwell.

141

But it also had its supporters.

Dear Lane, These Penguin Books are amazingly good value for money. If you can make the series pay for itself ~ with such books at such price ~ you will have performed a great publishing feat. Yours sincerely, J. B. Priestley.

'If a book is any good, the cheaper the better'. Bernard Shaw.

In 1937, Penguin moved to new offices and a warehouse at Harmondsworth, near the future Heathrow Airport and began to expand. 1937 also saw the launch of the Penguin Shakespeare series and the Pelican imprint ~ original non-fiction books on contemporary issues ~ and the appearance of a book-dispensing machine at Charing Cross called the Penguincubator.

As conflict in Europe drew closer, Penguin Specials such as What Hitler Wants achieved record-breaking sales. One of the best selling titles during the war was Aircraft Recognition, used by both civilians and the fighting forces to recognize enemy planes. Penguin also started an Armed Forces Book Club, bringing entertainment and comfort to soldiers cut off from friends and family.

"A Penguin could fit into a soldier's pocket or his kit bag ... It was especially prized in prison camps." Martin Bell.

Two of the company's most famous names were launched in the 1940s. Puffin was born in 1940 as a series of non-fiction picture books for children. They proved to be such a great success that Puffin started publishing fiction the following year, with Worzel Gummidge among its first titles. In 1946, Penguin Classics were launched with E. V. Rieu's translation of *The Odyssey*, making classic texts available to everyone.

INFORMATION FROM THE PENGUIN BOOK WEBSITE
ALLEN LANE, 'ALL ABOUT THE PENGUIN BOOKS',
THE BOOKSELLER, 22 MAY 1935
www.penguin.co.uk
Penguin cover images ~ Reproduced by permission of Penguin Books Ltd

To Aylesbury

*Train Line
to Stoke Mandeville
Hospital
Buckinghamshire*

AMERSHAM

HIGH
WYCOMBE

MAIDENHEAD

*Train Line
from Paddington
to Maidenhead*

DIARY LOCATIONS
LONDON, MAIDENHEAD, SCOTLAND AND SOMERSET

KINGS CROSS STATION: TERMINUS FOR THE EAST COAST MAIN LINE. LIVERPOOL ST: TERMINUS OF THE FORMER GREAT EASTERN RAILWAY, ORIGINALLY PROVIDING ROUTES TO NORWICH.

144

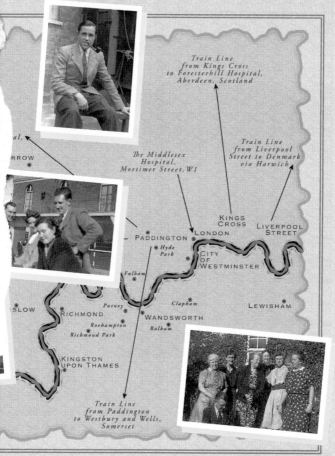

Train Line
from Kings Cross
to Foresterhill Hospital,
Aberdeen, Scotland

Train Line
from Liverpool
Street to Denmark
via Harwich

The Middlesex
Hospital,
Mortimer Street, W1

...al.

...RROW

KINGS
CROSS

LIVERPOOL
STREET

PADDINGTON London

Hyde
Park

CITY
OF
WESTMINSTER

Fulham

...SLOW RICHMOND Putney Clapham LEWISHAM

Roehampton WANDSWORTH
Richmond Park Balham

KINGSTON
UPON THAMES

Train Line
from Paddington
to Westbury and Wells,
Somerset

PADDINGTON STATION: TERMINUS OF THE GREAT WESTERN RAILWAY. VICTORIA PROVIDING
TRAIN SERVICES TO THE KENT COAST, MEDWAY TOWNS AND ROUTES TO SUSSEX.

145

PLACE NAMES

ENGLAND
Aldwych Corner
Aylesbury
Barnes
Bath
Cambridge
Chatham
Chipstead
Clapham Common
Covent Garden
Eastbourne
Frome
Hampton Court
Harwich
Kingston
Knightsbridge
London
Maidenhead
Manor Park
Marble Arch
Mortlake
Northwood
Northwood Hills
Oxford Street
Paddington
Putney
Reading
Ricky (Rickmansworth)
Somerset

Sonning
The Strand
Wedmore
Wells
Wembley Park
West Bradley
Westminster Bridge
Weston Super Mare
Wigmore Street

SCOTLAND
Aberdeen
Alford
Alltsigh
Ballachulish
Ballater
Balmaha
Balmoral
Ben Lomond
Ben Nevis
Braemars
Bridge of Don
Crianlarich
Cove
Deeside
Dee Street
Dunblane
Dundee
Echt

Edinburgh
Foresterhill
Fort Augustus
Fort William
Glasgow
Glencoe
Glen Nevis
Hazlehead
Hill of Fare
Inverbeg
Inverness
Inverurie
Kintore
Loch
Loch Lomond
Loch Ness
Loch Skene
Newcastle
Ross
Stirling
Stonehaven
Tomintoul

EUROPE
Arrbus
Assens
Borsgade
Bramminge
Christiansborg

Copenhagen
Den Gamle By
Denmark
Esbjerg
Elsinore
Germany
Horsens
Kobenhavn
Kolding
Koldinghus Castle
Korsfor
Korsfors
Little Belt Bridge
Malmo
Marselisborg
Nybeg
Odense
Ribe
Roskilde
Silkeborg
Sweden
Switzerland
The Old Town
Tivoli
Vejle

1946

The House on 92nd Street

The Wicked Lady

Caesar & Cleopatra/Odeon

Because of Him

Saratoga Trunk

Lady Windermeres Fan

Spellbound

The Common Touch & Come Live
with Me/Royal

Dragonwyck

Bedelia

The Elusive Lady/Wimbledon
Theatre/Mark Houston/Evelyn Laye

Grand National Night/Leslie
Banks/Apollo

I See a Dark Stranger

Captive Heart/Mr Ace

Overlanders

Their's is the Glory

Black Beauty

Stanley & Livingstone

Lord Mayors Show

The Sunballs (sic) ~ book

Wuthering Heights ~ book

1947

School for Secrets

Cakes & Ale

California

Swan Lake/Ballet

Dr Angelus/His Majesty's/Alastair Sim

Temptation Harbour/R. Newton

The Brothers

The Courtneys of Curzon St.

Stallion Road

Technicolour Wedding/Woman
in the Halls/Hippodrome

Off the Record/Piccadilly

Barber at Serville/Cambridge Theatre

Ideal Husband

1948

Spring in Park Lane

Chiltern Hundreds

Snowbound

Silver Wedding/Newsreel

Trade Show/Warner

London Belongs to Me

I remember Mama

D_ cold ~ DAMN COLD	N/D, N/D Ante Natal ~ NIGHT DUTY
b_ awful ~ BLOODY AWFUL	Mat. Maty. ~ MATERNITY
B_ cold ~ BLOODY COLD	GP's ~ GENERAL PRACTITIONERS
St. ~ STREET	NHS ~ NATIONAL HEALTH SERVICE
St., st. ~ STATION	P.T.S. ~ PRELIMINARY TRAINING
Co. ~ COMPANY	SCHOOL
Br. ~ BRIDGE	Webb J., Webb J & J Astor, ~ WEBB
back to town ~ LONDON	JOHNSON & JOHN ASTOR WARD
lbs ~ POUNDS IN WEIGHT	AT THE MIDDLESEX
Y.H. H.Y ~ YOUTH HOSTEL	Woola, 4th floor Woola ~
Hosp. bosp. ~ HOSPITAL	WOOLAVINGTON WING, WARD
Dr. ~ DOCTOR	AT THE MIDDLESEX
H/s ~ HOUSE SURGEON	M.V.H ~ MOUNT VERNON HOSPITAL
N/Sister ~ NIGHT SISTER	Queens X., Q.X. ~ QUEENS X,
S/N ~ STAFF NURSE	WARD AT FORESTERHILLS
S/ ~ SISTER	WWII ~ WORLD WAR II
Aft/aft ~ AFTERNOON	W.P.A.L ~ WAR TIME PERSONNEL
long aft. ~ LONG AFTERNOON	ALLOWANCE LIST
longs, ~ LENGTH OF DUTY/ON/OFF	D-day ~ THE D-DAY ALLIED
LA ~ LATES	LANDINGS ON THE BEACHES
Had a LA ~ HAD A LATE DUTY	OF NORMANDY IN NORTHERN FRANCE
Hrs/hr ~ HOURS, HOUR	AT THE START OF A MAJOR
m/d, md. ~ MIDDAY	OFFENSIVE AGAINST THE GERMANS
12 m/d ~ 12 MIDDAY	'V' Day ~ VICTORY IN EUROPE,
d/o ~ DAY OFF	GERMANY SURRENDERS
1/2 d, 1/2 day ~ HALF DAY	
w/k, W/k, w/k's ~ WEEKEND/ENDS	

Barbara Russell	BARB, babs
Lilian Russell, mother of Les, Jean & Barb	MOTHER
Walter Russell, father of Les, Jean & Barb	FATHER
Leslie Russell, elder brother of Barb	LES
Jean Russell, elder sister of Barb	JEAN
William Capon, husband of Jean	BILL
Alvin Ryall, wife of Les	PEG, PEGGY
Aunt Blanche, close family friend	A,B., A. BLANCHE
Nancy Hole, daughter of Winifred &	NANCE
William Hole of Swansea, niece of Unc	
Tom Hole, husband of Lil	UNC
Lilian Blackstock, wife of Tom	A.LIL, AUNT LIL
Family pet of Nance, A. Lil & Unc	POOH
friend of Unc	MR RUSHTON
relations of the Hole/Wall family	AUNTS
relation of the Hole/Wall family	A. KATE
Peg's mother	AUNTY WYN
Peg's father	UNCLE ERN
Peg's grandmother	NANA
Joyce Clark, close friend of Barb	JOYCE
June Clark, sister of Joyce	JUNE HILL
Cousins of Joyce & June	MARGERY & DOREEN
Peter Cocking, friend of Les	PETER
friend of the Russells	REG
friends of Barb & Joyce	SAM & CECIL
relatives/friends of Peg	CLARE & LITTLE ANGELA

Every care has been taken to trace copyright holders but any omissions will, if notified, be corrected in any future edition.

1904 - 1936 Poems, Lord Gorell. First Edition, 1937
Published by John Murray. London *(page v).*

Chronology of British History, Copyright 1995 Geddes & Grossett Ltd, Brockhampton Reference/Press. London *(pages 183-193, 1939/1949).*

A Concise History of England, F E Haliday, Published in 1964 by Thames & Hudson. Department of Health, Government UK website: www.gov.uk
Health Services before 1948: www.nhs.uk

The Middlesex Hospital, Hilary St. George Saunders. First Edition published in 1949 by Max Parrish & Co Limited. London *(pages 19-21).*

The Middlesex Hospital. The names of the wards and the story they tell. C D Shaw & W E Winterton. Published in 1983 by The Friends of The Middlesex Hospital. Line drawing image/front cover.

Preliminary Training School Records. Trust Archivist, UCLH NHS, 250 Euston Road, NW1 2PG. Archives at UCL: www.uclh.nhs.uk
Hospital Records Database, The National Archives/www.nationalarchives.gov.uk

General Register Office Certificates: Births, Deaths & Marriages.

Illustrated Family Medical Encyclopaedia, 1975. Third revision, 1977. Published by The Readers Digest Association Limited. London *(page 347).*
Principles of Medicine and Medical Nursing, J C Houston and Marion Stockdale, Fourth Edition revised by J C Houston and Hilary Hyde White, SRN, 1975. Published by Hodder & Stoughton. London *(pages 55-62).*
Pulmonary Tuberculosis ~ Originally by Frederick Marais. www.ukcoalition.org/tb/history.html

'Class of '48', article and image from The Daily Mail relating to the Olympic Games held in London in 1948.

'All About the Penguin Books', Allen Lane The Bookseller, 22 May 1935. Penguin cover images ~ Reproduced by permission of Penguin Books Ltd. www.penguin.co.uk